WITCH
HUNT

Also by Michael Dorman

CONFRONTATION—Politics and Protest

THE GEORGE WALLACE MYTH

KING OF THE COURTROOM

THE MAKING OF A SLUM

PAYOFF—The Role of
Organized Crime in American Politics

THE SECOND MAN—The Changing
Role of the Vice Presidency

THE SECRET SERVICE STORY

UNDER 21: A Young People's
Guide to Legal Rights

VESCO—The Infernal
Money-Making Machine

WE SHALL OVERCOME

MICHAEL DORMAN

★ ★ ★ ★ ★

WITCH HUNT

The Underside of American Democracy

Delacorte Press / New York

Manufactured in the United States of America

First printing

Library of Congress Cataloging in Publication Data

Dorman, Michael.
Witch hunt.

Bibliography: p.
Includes index.
SUMMARY: Traces government investigations of
communist and subversive activities in the United States.
1. Civil rights—United States—Juvenile literature. 2.
Loyalty-security program, 1947- —Juvenile literature.
3. Watergate Affair, 1972- —Juvenile literature. [1.
Anti-communist movement. 2. United States. Congress.
House. Committee on Un-American activities. 3. Civil
rights] I. Title.
JC599.U5D67   323.4'0973   75-32917
ISBN 0-440-09689-8

For the Reverend Douglas E. Bartlett
—a dedicated civil libertarian,
a fighter of good fights,
and a loyal friend.

CONTENTS

INTRODUCTION

Witch hunt—an intensive effort to discover and expose disloyalty, subversion, dishonesty or the like, usually based on slight, doubtful or irrelevant evidence.
—The American College Dictionary

On August 9, 1974, when Gerald Ford took the oath as president upon the resignation of Richard Nixon, he declared to the American people that "our long national nightmare is over." Ford referred, of course, to the Watergate scandal—which had driven Nixon from office in disgrace.

Many people think of Watergate merely in terms of the burglary at the Democratic National Headquarters carried out by men hired by Nixon's 1972 reelection organization. But the Watergate affair was far more significant than any one illegal act, such as the burglary. In its broadest sense, Watergate represented a series of events adding up to the most insidious political witch hunt in the nation's history.

Marshaling the massive power within the White House and the numerous agencies of the executive branch, Nixon launched a reign of terror against his political enemies. Secret investigations, using such means as illegal wiretaps and burglaries, sought information that could be used to portray opposition politicians, critical newsmen, and dissident citizens as traitors. White House officials compiled lists of Nixon enemies with the intention of having them harassed by the Internal Revenue Service and other government agencies. The legitimate roles of the FBI and CIA were perverted as agents were ordered to compile secret dossiers on Americans who had committed no crimes but were considered "disloyal" to the Nixon administration. And all of this was done in the name of preserving national security when, in fact, its intention was merely to preserve the political power of the Nixon regime.

In many ways, these events followed the classic pattern of the American political witch hunt. They depended on the questionable assumption that many Americans—including nationally prominent political figures—were either disloyal to their country or serving as dupes of "subversive" groups. Further, they relied on the premise that drastic (even illegal) means were necessary to purge such "un-American" elements from the land.

This is not a book about Watergate, but rather about the broader subject of the history of American political witch hunts. Still, it seems appropriate to mention Watergate prominently at the outset, for, as will be seen, the Watergate affair grew out of an aura of political suspicion that had been nurtured for decades. And, as will also be seen, Richard Nixon was a product of the witch-hunt era. He first came to national prominence as a congressional witch hunter during the early 1950s. If it had not been for that role, he probably would never have reached the White House.

Long before he was elected president, it was clear that Nixon—almost by nature—suspected the worst of his political opponents. As the now-defunct *Reporter* magazine once put it: "Mr. Nixon's experience in politics must have been disillusioning for a clean-cut American boy, because everybody he has ever campaigned against has turned out, on his investigation, to be linked to something sinister." That sort of distrust is symptomatic of political witch hunters, past and present.

Despite President Ford's statement that "our long national nightmare is over," the problems exposed during the Watergate affair did not dissolve with his inauguration. Many of them remain with us as the nation continues to suffer the effects of the witch-hunt philosophy at work. Thus, it seems appropriate to examine the entire history of American political witch hunts—with emphasis on facts that are relevant today.

Use of the term "witch hunt" throughout the book does not imply that every governmental or private investigation of alleged subversion is a witch hunt. That is far from the case. But in many instances, legitimate investigations have been permitted to stray across the fine line separating appropriate inquiry from intimidation.

This book is not intended to espouse any political cause —much less the cause of extremist groups. It is written in the hope that it will shed light on a subject of essential importance to Americans who value their freedom of expression and association. The First Amendment, which guarantees freedom of speech and assembly, does not apply merely to those who hold orthodox views; it applies to all Americans. The same is true of the Fifth Amendment, which protects citizens from being forced to testify against themselves. As the late Supreme Court Justice Hugo Black wrote: "Centuries of experience testify that laws aimed at one political . . . group, however rational these laws may be in their beginnings, generate hatreds and prejudices which spread rapidly beyond control."

In these tumultuous times, many hatreds and prejudices seem "beyond control." The present generation of young Americans will soon find itself confronted with a challenge —whether to adopt the cynicism and suspicion of the witch-hunt era or forge a new path of true liberty of belief and expression. In facing that challenge, young people might do well to consider the words of the late distinguished jurist Learned Hand. Addressing the Board of Regents of the State University of New York in 1954, during a period of intense witch-hunt activities, Judge Hand said:

> I had rather take my chance that some traitors will escape detection than spread abroad a spirit of general suspicion and distrust, which accepts rumor and gossip in place of undismayed and unintimidated inquiry. . . . That community is already in the process of dissolution where each man begins to eye his neighbor as a possible enemy; where non-conformity with the accepted creed, political as well as religious, is a mark of disaffection; where denunciation, without specification or backing, takes the place of evidence; where faith in the eventual supremacy of reason has become so timid that we dare not enter our convictions in the open lists, to win or lose.

MICHAEL DORMAN
Dix Hills, New York

1

★ ★ ★

An Innocent Victim

On March 11, 1954, a bewildered woman named Annie Lee Moss walked into a Senate hearing room in the United States Capitol, blinked into the unaccustomed glare of television lights, and raised her right hand. Senator Joseph R. McCarthy, a controversial Wisconsin Republican heading a widely publicized investigation of alleged subversion in the federal government, asked her: "Do you swear to tell the truth, the whole truth and nothing but the truth—so help you God?"

"I do," Mrs. Moss replied.

Until that moment, hardly anyone in the country had heard of Annie Lee Moss. She was an obscure, poorly educated woman who had held a minor job as a civilian employee of the United States Army in Washington, D.C. Now, through none of her own doing, she had suddenly been catapulted into the national spotlight.

McCarthy, often accused of making charges that he could not prove, was responsible for Mrs. Moss's predicament. In an attempt to convince the public that the government was "coddling" subversives, he had accused Mrs. Moss of being a member of the Communist Party. He claimed to be horrified that a known communist should be employed as a "code clerk" at the Pentagon, supposedly handling "topmost" secret messages. Although McCarthy provided no proof of his allegations, the army suspended Mrs. Moss from her job. She was then ordered to testify before a televised hearing of McCarthy's investigating committee.

There, it quickly became clear that Mrs. Moss was not a code clerk and that she did not have access to military secrets. She merely operated a machine that transmitted coded messages—a job that gave her no knowledge of the messages themselves. Mrs. Moss testified that her job gave her no access to the Pentagon code room, that she knew nothing about code secrets, and that she had never heard of such government classifications as "confidential," "secret," and "top secret." In fact, for a large part of her employment by the army, she had not even operated the transmitting machine; she had worked in the Pentagon cafeteria.

By the time Mrs. Moss had given that testimony, it seemed clear that McCarthy's "case" against her was woefully inadequate. But McCarthy pressed on, apparently hoping he could avoid further embarrassment by at least proving that Mrs. Moss was indeed a communist.

There was no evidence, however, to support such an assumption. Throughout the questioning, Mrs. Moss testified that she had never been a member of the Communist Party, nor had she paid dues to it.

A member of McCarthy's committee, Democratic Senator Stuart Symington of Missouri, finally grew impatient

with the treatment being given Mrs. Moss. He interrupted the hostile questioning and asked her: "Did you
ever hear of Karl Marx?"

Mrs. Moss, appearing puzzled, replied: "Who's that?"

Spectators in the hearing room burst into laughter. If
Mrs. Moss did not even recognize the name of Karl Marx,
the chief theorist of modern socialism and communism,
it seemed unlikely that she was a member of the Communist Party.

Senator Symington continued the questioning: "Would
you ever do anything to hurt your country?"

"No, sir," Mrs. Moss replied.

"Have you ever had any information that you received
in your job that you passed on to anybody about these
codes?" he asked her.

"No, sir," she answered.

"Has anybody ever asked you to join the Communist
Party?"

"No, sir. If they had, I would have reported it."

"What are you living on now? Have you got any
savings?"

"No, sir," Mrs. Moss said. She explained that she had
just about run out of money since being suspended from
her job. Unless the army allowed her to return to work
soon, she would be forced to go on welfare. By that point,
Senator McCarthy, apparently recognizing that his charges
against Mrs. Moss had boomeranged, suddenly remembered
he had "an important appointment" and left the hearing
room. The hearing continued, however, and Senator
Symington told Mrs. Moss: "I may be sticking my neck
out, but I think you are telling the truth."

"I certainly am," Mrs. Moss said.

"If you are not taken back by the army, you come

around and see me and I am going to see that you get a job," Symington told her.

A short time later, Mrs. Moss was excused from the witness chair. In the end, she was restored to her job at the Pentagon. But the fact remained that she had been suspended from the job and accused before a national television audience of being a communist—without any apparent justification. And unfortunately, as Mrs. Moss would later learn, unsubstantiated accusations of subversive activity can produce damaging effects even after they are discredited. Some citizens tend to remember the accusations better than the refutations. Thus, the harm inflicted by a false accusation of subversion can never be totally undone. As Senator Charles E. Potter, a Michigan Republican who served on the McCarthy committee, wrote of Mrs. Moss: "The pattern of her life had been permanently damaged."

The case of Annie Lee Moss represented a classic example of the American political witch hunt: "slight, doubtful or irrelevant evidence" had been used to try to punish her for what were presumed to be her unpopular political beliefs. In her case, it appeared that she did not even hold such beliefs. But in many other witch-hunt cases, attempts were made—often successfully—to "expose" and penalize Americans for sincerely held but unorthodox political sentiments.

Senator McCarthy was considered the most notorious of the congressional witch hunters. He tossed allegations around so recklessly that the term "McCarthyism" was coined to refer to all manner of irresponsible investigations. Today, when the term "McCarthy era" is used, it refers to the period in the 1950s when the senator was at the height of his power. But at various times in

American history, other witch hunters have resorted to similar tactics.

During the 1930s, 1940s, and 1950s—a period of domestic turmoil that spawned numerous witch hunts—countless lives were scarred by ill-founded, irresponsible, or exaggerated charges of political subversion. Waves of near-hysteria swept through many areas of the country. It became a cliché, but was nonetheless true, that large numbers of Americans saw communists and their sympathizers "hiding under every bed." Self-appointed vigilantes spied on their neighbors in the hope of discovering "traitors" in their midst.

The congressional committee compiled lists of thousands of persons with suspect backgrounds. Once a person's name appeared on such a list, he became subject to all manner of harassment. He might be fired from his job. He might find his home vandalized. He and members of his family might be physically assaulted by self-styled "one-hundred-percent Americans." They might be shunned by their neighbors. The children in the family might be taunted as "commies" and "traitors" by their schoolmates. Some industries, such as those involved in producing motion pictures and television and radio shows, maintained blacklists barring the employment of persons with supposedly subversive or even "controversial" backgrounds.

At the heart of the witch-hunt movement were several congressional committees that conducted seemingly interminable hearings into the purported menace posed by subversives. Often, men and women who had flirted briefly with communism or other unpopular political causes twenty to thirty years earlier were summoned before the committees and compelled to confess their youthful indiscretions at televised hearings. The committees were

[5]

not satisfied merely to hear the witnesses recount their own experiences, but insisted that they also identify and testify about all other persons who had been involved with them in supposedly subversive organizations. Many witnesses found repugnant the demands that they become informers against former associates, who often had abandoned their questionable activities many years earlier. But if the witnesses refused to identify the associates, they ran the risk of being imprisoned on charges of "contempt" of Congress—the willful disregard of the authority of the legislative body.

However, much of the testimony before the investigating committees was provided by virtual professional witnesses—former communists who spent a large part of their time appearing at hearings in which they purported to "expose" persons they identified as their former associates. Such witnesses received expense money and sometimes even fees from the committee. In addition, some of them—as a result of the publicity received from their testimony—began earning sizable fees for lecturing about their experiences and "the communist menace." Naturally, such witnesses had vested interests in continuing to be called for testimony before the committees. There was constant pressure on them to provide fresh revelations and new names for the witch-hunt lists. Under such circumstances, some witnesses resorted to exaggeration or to outright lies in the attempt to provide the sort of sensational testimony the committees apparently wanted to hear.

In addition to congressional committees, other government agencies regularly conducted investigations of alleged subversive activities. There was the FBI, of course, and there were also a number of loyalty-review boards responsi-

[6]

ble for checking on the backgrounds of persons employed (or seeking employment) either by the federal government or by private industries awarded government contracts. During the early 1950s, almost 10,000,000 Americans were subject to such clearance. In more recent years, both congressional committees and agencies of the executive branch have continued to perpetuate this witch-hunt philosophy.

How did all of this begin? How did a nation purporting to guarantee freedom of expression and assembly allow itself to fall into a quagmire of suppression and suspicion? To answer those questions, we must take a backward glance at the political history of the Republic.

SOURCES AND SUPPLEMENTARY READING

Additional information on the Annie Lee Moss case can be found in *The Nightmare Decade* by Fred J. Cook (Random House, 1971) and *Days of Shame* by Charles E. Potter (Coward, McCann and Geoghegan, 1965).

General background information on the witch-hunt era appears in such books as *The Loyalty of Free Men* by Alan Barth (Viking, 1951); *But We Were Born Free* by Elmer Davis (Bobbs-Merrill, 1954); *The Un-Americans* by Frank J. Donner (Ballantine, 1961); *When Even Angels Wept* by Lately Thomas (William Morrow, 1973); and *Grand Inquest* by Telford Taylor (Simon and Schuster, 1955).

2
★ ★ ★

The Origins of
Congressional Investigations

The United States Constitution contains no provision specifically authorizing Congress to conduct investigations. Yet, both the House and Senate have carried out investigations almost since the founding of the Republic.

The first congressional investigation in the nation's history was launched in 1792, three years after George Washington's inauguration as president. It concerned a disastrous military campaign undertaken by the United States Army in 1791. The mission was intended to neutralize Indians who had been terrorizing settlers along the frontier in what is now Ohio. A force of about 1,500 soldiers, under the command of Major General Arthur St. Clair, was assigned the job. Many of the men were raw recruits with virtually no training. The entire force's equipment was inadequate; much of its gunpowder was defective.

Part of General St. Clair's mission involved building fortifications to protect the settlers between Fort Washington (on the site of present-day Cincinnati) and several Indian villages to the north. The soldiers' march toward the headwaters of the Wabash River was plagued by rainy, cold weather, and many of the men became dispirited. On October 30, 1791, while the troops were still en route, about sixty of the recruits suddenly claimed that the period of their enlistment had expired. They deserted their ranks and began making their way back. General St. Clair sent a regiment of his best troops to round up the deserters, but meanwhile kept pressing forward with the remainder of his soldiers.

By November 3, neither the round-up regiment nor the deserters had rejoined the main force. St. Clair decided to camp for the night on a piece of high ground along the east branch of the upper Wabash River near the current site of Fort Recovery, Ohio. When the sun came up, the remaining troops were suddenly subjected to a surprise attack by a massive force of Shawnee, Miami, and Delaware Indians. Although the soldiers displayed great courage, their lack of training and poor equipment prevented them from battling the Indians on anything approaching even terms. The battle resulted in a rout of the troops, with more than 600 men killed and more than 300 wounded. St. Clair himself had three horses shot out from under him, but escaped injury.

He managed to lead the surviving soldiers back to the safety of a military post, Fort Jefferson, about thirty miles south of the battle scene. In view of the heavy casualties his troops had suffered, St. Clair decided against renewing the battle with the Indians. He took his men back to Fort Washington, where he left them under the command of his subordinates. Then he set out for Philadelphia, which was the nation's capital at the time, to report on the military defeat to President Washington.

During the trip to Philadelphia, St. Clair became aware that he was being sharply criticized in many quarters because of the catastrophic mission. It was not the first time in his military career that he had been subjected to public disapproval. During the Revolutionary War, he had commanded the colonial troops at Fort Ticonderoga, New York. When he found his men vastly outnumbered by an advancing force of British troops led by General John Burgoyne, St. Clair ordered the fort evacuated. Although his decision seemed justified, it was assailed by many critics, who accused him of cowardice. Stung by the criticism, St. Clair demanded that a court-martial be convened to investigate his conduct at Fort Ticonderoga. The court-martial completely cleared him, ruling that he had commanded "with highest honor."

As St. Clair traveled to Philadelphia, it occurred to him that he might again be able to clear his name by the same means he had used before. When he saw President Washington, he requested that a court-martial be convened to investigate the circumstances of the Indian battle. Although Washington sympathized with St. Clair and felt he was being unjustly blamed for the defeat, he rejected the request on the ground that there were not enough army officers of sufficiently high rank available to form a military court competent to judge the conduct of a major general.

Meanwhile, the furor over the incident continued to grow. In the House of Representatives, a proposal was introduced calling upon the president to conduct an investigation of St. Clair's ill-fated mission. But some congressmen argued that the Constitution's provision for a separation of powers among the executive, legislative, and judicial branches of government would be violated by the proposal—since it involved an attempt by the House to direct the president's operation of the executive branch. The proposal was defeated. In its place, a new measure was introduced under which the House itself would appoint a special committee to investigate the affair. There was ample precedent for the creation of such a committee; both the English Parliament and American colonial legislatures had often appointed investigating committees in the past. On March 27, 1792, the House voted to name a select committee "to inquire into the failure of the late expedition under General St. Clair."

Thus began the long history of congressional investigations in the United States. The investigating committee members were empowered "to call for such persons, papers and records as may be necessary to assist in their inquiries." They promptly wrote to Secretary of War Henry Knox, asking him to produce all orders, records, and correspondence concerning St. Clair's expedition. Knox referred the request to President Washington, who called a cabinet meeting to consider both the immediate and long-range implications. Washington recognized that an important precedent would be set by the manner in which the executive branch responded to the congressional request for its records. He asked the cabinet to consider first whether the House committee had a legitimate right to conduct such an investigation and, if so, whether the executive branch was obliged to turn over its records to the committee.

The cabinet decided that the committee was indeed entitled to carry out the investigation. It also determined that the executive branch should turn over any requested documents whose disclosure would serve the public interest; but any documents whose disclosure would endanger the public interest should be withheld. That last decision laid the groundwork for various presidents' refusal to turn over certain confidential records to Congress under the doctrine of "executive privilege"—a concept that remains controversial at this writing.

In the St. Clair case, Washington decided to turn all the requested documents over to the congressional committee. St. Clair, testifying before the committee, blamed the military defeat on the poor training given his soldiers before their assignment to his command and on the shoddy equipment provided them. Other witnesses called to testify before the committee included Secretary of War Knox and the army's quartermaster, Samuel Hodgdon, who had been in charge of supplying the equipment to St. Clair's troops. Both denied any responsibility for the military defeat.

The committee found that "gross mismanagements and neglects" by the War Department and the quartermaster had been the chief causes of the defeat. On May 8, 1792, it issued a unanimous report completely clearing St. Clair of blame.

The committee report was then subject to approval by the entire House. But since the report was issued on the final day of a congressional session, House action was put off until a new session convened six months later. During the intervening period, allies of Secretary of War Knox did everything possible to create opposition to the report among House members. Largely as a result of such lobbying activities, the House refused to approve the report when Congress reconvened, and sent it back to the committee for further study. The committee permitted Knox and Hodgdon to file long written critiques of the original report. St. Clair then filed answers to the critiques. Ultimately, the committee prepared a revised report that softened the charges against the War Department and the quartermaster but continued to blame them for the defeat. In February 1793, however, the House set the report aside without approving or disapproving it. The matter thus was officially permitted to die without providing St. Clair the full justification he had sought.

The blot on St. Clair's reputation continued to dog him throughout his life. At several stages during his military and governmental careers, he had advanced his own money to pay government debts—fully expecting to be reimbursed. But when he tried to get Congress to appropriate money to repay him, he encountered opposition based on the old accusations regarding the military defeat. Meanwhile, St. Clair's creditors sued to collect money he owed and forced him to sell his home to satisfy the debts. He was then reduced to living in a tiny log cabin and scraping out a bare existence as a small-time merchant. It was not until 1818, when St. Clair was eighty-four, that Congress finally agreed to fulfill its financial obligation by paying him a monthly pension of sixty dollars. He collected the pension for only six months, however, before dying from injuries suffered in a fall from a horse-drawn wagon.

Although the House committee investigation of the St. Clair affair did not provide a conclusive ending, it set an important precedent in establishing the power of congressional committees to conduct investigations. In the years that followed, congressional investigations became accepted as integral parts of the legislative process. Among the more prominent investigations conducted by congressional committees were those involving the Treasury

[13]

Department in 1800 and 1824; the administration of the territorial government of Mississippi in 1800; General Andrew Jackson's leadership during the Seminole Wars in Florida in 1818; the Post Office Department in 1820, 1822, and 1830; the Internal Revenue Bureau in 1828; the Bank of the United States in 1832 and 1834; the New York Custom House in 1839; the commissioner of Indian affairs in 1849; the secretary of the interior in 1850; John Brown's raid on Harpers Ferry in 1859; military operations during the Civil War; railroad scandals in 1873; the civil service in 1888 and 1897; the General Land Office in 1897; use of third-degree questioning methods by government officials in 1910; and Justice Department scandals and the Teapot Dome scandal, involving government oil reserves, in 1924.

Periodically during these years, various congressional investigations were permitted to deteriorate into witch hunts. But the major period of congressional witch hunting and public fear began during the 1930s. That is not to say, however, that all or even most congressional investigations after the 1930s amounted to witch hunts. Quite to the contrary, most of them were legitimate and valuable inquiries in which the constitutional rights of those under investigation were protected. Former President Harry S Truman first came to national attention, for example, through his even-handed service as chairman of a Senate committee that investigated the nation's defense program early in World War II. Similarly, Democratic Senator Estes Kefauver of Tennessee achieved national prominence during the 1950s as chairman of a committee that exposed the secret workings of organized-crime syndicates—including their connections with corrupt politicians and police officials. Kefauver also rendered valuable

[14]

service by heading an investigation of monopolistic practices within the drug industry. Later, a committee headed by Democratic Senator John McClellan of Arkansas and also including then-Senator John F. Kennedy of Massachusetts exposed numerous acts of corruption involving union officials and businessmen. Other committees of the Senate and House uncovered important scandals within the administrations of Presidents Truman, Dwight D. Eisenhower, and Lyndon B. Johnson. And of course, congressional committees played major roles in the investigation of the Watergate scandal during President Richard Nixon's administration.

Side by side with such investigations as these, however, the nation witnessed the increasing development of congressional inquiries that had the unmistakable characteristics of witch hunts. It was perhaps inevitable that such a trend should have begun reaching significant proportions during the 1930s, when the Depression had thrown millions out of work. Many disillusioned citizens expressed their support for alternate systems of government—such as communism, socialism and fascism. Various radical groups sprang up throughout the country. The activities of such organizations alarmed many Americans, who saw them as threats to the survival of "the American way of life." From Capitol Hill came repeated warnings that something had to be done to curb alleged "subversion."

SOURCES AND SUPPLEMENTARY READING

Telford Taylor's *Grand Inquest* contains an excellent discussion of the British parliamentary inquiry system that laid the groundwork for American congressional

[15]

investigations. Taylor also discusses in detail the case of General Arthur St. Clair and how it established precedents that would affect later congressional investigations.

Murray Kempton's *Part of Our Time* (Simon and Schuster, 1955) is a highly readable and moving discussion of the political, social, and economic forces of the thirties as symbolized by some of that era's most controversial Americans. The book captures well the spirit of the period, a time that was ripe for the witch-hunt movement.

3
★ ★ ★
Martin Dies
Turns Witch Hunter

On a warm spring day several years ago, in the small town of Lufkin in the piney woods of the east Texas hill country, I spent a leisurely day interviewing a country lawyer named Martin Dies. At six-foot-three and 210 pounds, with his broad-brimmed hat cocked at a jaunty angle, Dies seemed the prototype of the soft-spoken but leather-tough Texan. One who knew little of his background would have been unlikely to suspect that Dies had once been the scourge of Capitol Hill. As the first of the major congressional witch hunters, he remained a controversial figure even to his death in 1972.

At the time of the interview, Dies had been retired from Congress for a decade. He had mellowed somewhat during that period, and conceded that he had made mistakes as chairman of the House Un-American Activities Committee (HUAC). But all in all, he insisted that the committee had rendered valuable service in routing out communists: "The fact is that ninety percent of our

[17]

findings about the communists have been verified," Dies said. "When I warned about communists in government, . . . my views were regarded as fantastic. Well, I have been vindicated."

Some observers considered Dies a hero—the first congressional figure to investigate the "communist menace." But many others agreed with the comment of the late President· Franklin D. Roosevelt that the operation of HUAC, under Dies's leadership, had amounted to a "sordid procedure." In either case, it can be said that the work of the Dies committee set the tone for many of the witch hunts that were to follow.

Martin Dies—an ambitious, young conservative Democratic congressman who entered the House in 1931—was desperately searching for some subject on which he could head an investigating committee. He had noted with envy the manner in which other members of Congress had become nationally prominent through their leadership of such committees. After unsuccessfully proposing that Congress investigate such matters as the resignation of government officials to take high-paying corporate jobs, purported government violations of freedom of the press, and charges that the nation was controlled by sixty wealthy families, Dies finally struck on the issue of subversion.

In 1938, he introduced in the House a resolution calling for creation of a special committee to investigate

> . . . the extent, character and object of un-American propaganda activities in the United States; the diffusion within the United States of subversive and un-American propaganda that is instigated from foreign countries or of a domestic origin and attacks the principle of the form of government as guaranteed

by the Constitution; and all other questions in relation thereto that would aid Congress in any necessary remedial legislation.

The proposal touched off spirited opposition from some members of the House. Dies's fellow Texas Democrat, liberal Congressman Maury Maverick, charged that the measure would give the proposed committee "blanket powers to investigate, humiliate, meddle with anything and everything." When several congressmen asked for a definition of the term "un-American," Maverick shouted: "Un-American! Un-American is simply something that somebody else does not agree to."

Some supporters of the resolution argued that the proposed committee was intended to investigate subversives of the right wing as well as the left wing, Nazis as well as communists. But the most telling argument seemed to be made by one congressman who conceded: "I do not want to be accused of refusing to vote for legislation to investigate un-American activities."

Finally, on May 26, 1938, the House voted by 191 to 41 to establish the committee. Under the terms of the resolution, as a special committee (rather than a standing committee of the House), it was supposed to complete its work and go out of existence before the next Congress convened seven months later, in January 1939. But in fact, it never went out of business. It has continued to function under one name or another, in one government department or another, despite frequent attempts by critics to abolish it.

Not surprisingly, Martin Dies was named as the first chairman. He was then only thirty-seven, and hoped to use the committee chairmanship as a springboard for an eventual race for a Senate seat. He also hoped to employ it as a forum for his stiff opposition to many of the New Deal programs of President Franklin D. Roosevelt. Also appointed to the committee were four other Democrats (Joe Starnes of Alabama, Harold Mosier of Ohio, John Dempsey of New Mexico, and Arthur Healey of Massachusetts) and two Republicans (J. Parnell Thomas of New Jersey and Noah Mason of Illinois). In August 1938, as the committee was about to begin investigative hearings, Dies issued a statement in which he promised to avoid witch hunts and "character assassination."

Just one day after issuing the statement, however, Dies permitted the committee hearings to be used as a forum for precisely the sort of smears he had promised to avoid. It was the first of many such smears to be delivered either by witnesses before the committee or by the committee itself. In the witness chair was John P. Frey, president of the Metal Trades Department of the American Federation of Labor. At the time, the AFL was engaged in a bitter rivalry with the Congress of Industrial Organizations. (It would not be before 1955 that the two labor organizations would merge into the AFL-CIO.)

Without offering a shred of corroborating evidence, Frey testified that the CIO was dominated by communists. He identified scores of CIO unions that he claimed were controlled by communists, and read into the committee record the names of 283 CIO organizers he contended were card-carrying members of the Communist Party. Frey testified that communism had made no headway in the United States until the organization of the CIO, but "since then the Communist Party has become a definite factor in the American labor movement." His

[20]

testimony was accepted unquestionably by Dies and the committee members. He was not asked to provide any proof for his charges.

Frey's testimony produced front-page headlines across the country, yet none of the 283 persons named was given the opportunity to appear before the committee and deny the charges. Many of those accused were quickly fired by their employers and blacklisted by other companies. They and others like them who would be charged with subversive activities in later hearings had virtually no legal recourse against their accusers. Libel and slander laws provide that nobody can win a suit over a statement made about him in an official proceeding such as a legislative hearing or a court trial.

Frey was followed by Walter S. Steele, chairman of the American Coalition Committee on National Security, which described itself as a confederation of 114 "patriotic" organizations. Steele was the first of many self-appointed "patriots" (critics called them vigilantes) who would appear voluntarily before the committee over the years and deliver broad-scale allegations of subversion against individuals and organizations they disliked. In two days of testimony, he placed in the committee record the names of 641 organizations he charged were communist dominated. Among them were the Boy Scouts and the Camp Fire Girls, both of which Steele said were being led astray by persons who claimed to be interested in promoting international understanding. Although some of Steele's charges produced belly laughs from spectators, they were received with great solemnity by committee members.

As in Frey's case, Steele's testimony produced a fresh wave of newspaper headlines. A pattern that would be followed in the press for years was established with the testimony of these two witnesses. Sensational charges would be made before the committee, often timed to meet newspaper deadlines. Reporters, making little or no effort to obtain comment from those accused, would rush into print with the allegations. By the time the accused had their say, their remarks—if published at all—would often be buried inconspicuously on inside pages. Meanwhile, the front pages would be plastered with new allegations against still other persons. Martin Dies, who had wanted to head an investigating committee so that he could attract national publicity and attention, got a heady taste of both as a result of the Frey and Steele testimony.

Although Dies had promised to investigate right-wing organizations along with those of the left, the committee made only a quick pass at fulfilling the pledge. A few witnesses were called to describe the threat posed by American Nazis and their sympathizers, but then the subject was quickly forgotten. The "political gold mine"—as it was called by news analyst Kenneth Crawford—appeared to be in "exposing" alleged communists.

Among the targets the committee chose for major investigation in late 1938 was the Federal Theatre Project of the Works Progress Administration. President Roosevelt, as one of his measures aimed at pulling the nation out of the Depression, had established the WPA to put many of the unemployed to work on government projects. As part of this program, the Federal Theatre Project employed several thousand writers, actors, actresses, and other personnel. It presented more than a thousand productions throughout the country over a period of several years —chiefly free performances before spectators who had never seen a professional production.

[22]

Congressman Dies, and some other members of his committee who shared his distaste for the New Deal programs, saw the theater project as a perfect mark for an attack on the Roosevelt administration. With the country struggling to fight its way out of economic chaos, they reasoned that the government had more urgent needs than to pour money into an entertainment program. Besides, the committee members did not like the type of plays being produced by the theater project. As Congressman J. Parnell Thomas put it before the committee had even opened its hearings: "Practically every play presented under the auspices of the project is sheer propaganda for communism or the New Deal." He claimed the project was dominated by communists.

There undoubtedly were some communists employed in the theater project, but their numbers and influence were grossly overstated by committee members. The committee tried to prove that virtually any reference to controversial social issues in plays produced by the theater project constituted evidence of communist propaganda. The national director of the theater project, Mrs. Hallie Flanagan, was subjected to severe harassment by committee members when she testified at the hearings in December 1938.

Before taking her government job, Mrs. Flanagan had established herself as a distinguished figure in the American theater. A playwright, she had been the first American woman to win a Guggenheim Foundation fellowship. She had later become a professor of English and director of the Experimental Theater at Vassar College. A previous witness had told the committee: "I cannot prove that Mrs. Flanagan has Communist [Party] membership. . . . But I can prove . . . that her communist sympathies,

[23]

tendencies and methods of organization are being used in the Federal Theatre Project." Although the witness did not provide the promised proof, her allegations went unchallenged by committee members.

When Mrs. Flanagan took the witness chair, she denied harboring sympathies for the communist cause:

> . . . I am an American and I believe in American democracy. I believe the Works Progress Administration is one great bulwark of that democracy. I believe the Federal Theatre, which is one small part of that large pattern, is honestly trying in every way possible to interpret the best interests of the people of this democracy. I am not in sympathy with any other form of government in this country.

Committee members questioned her closely about the fact that, while traveling on her Guggenheim Foundation fellowship eleven years earlier, one of the twelve countries she had visited had been Russia. They dredged up old quotations from articles and interviews by Mrs. Flanagan, such as one in which she described the Russian theater as "live and vital."

At another point, she was questioned about an article she had written in which she had referred to the famed English playwright Christopher Marlowe. Congressman Joe Starnes, obviously no authority on the theater said: "You are quoting from this Marlowe. Is he a communist?"

Throughout the hearings, committee members took the position that not only out-and-out communist propaganda but any material dealing with class consciousness was improper in plays produced by the Federal Theatre Project. They accused Mrs. Flanagan of allowing the project to stage plays emphasizing the differences among various classes of Americans and casting the working class in the most favorable light. Mrs. Flanagan denied the charge and said that only ten percent of the project's plays dealt with social and economic issues.

Individual project plays that expressed ideas unpopular with committee members were subjected to close scrutiny at the hearings. One such play, *Power*, advocated public ownership of electrical power facilities. Public versus private ownership of power facilities was a controversial issue at the time. The Tennessee Valley Authority, a federal project that provided cheap electrical power, was in its infancy and was being criticized by some as "socialistic." Its critics predicted that it would lead to additional government ventures in providing power, at the expense of private enterprise.

During the hearing, Chairman Dies and the committee continued to bear down on the question of public ownership. In her testimony, Mrs. Flanagan held to the point that plays were chosen on the basis of their intrinsic quality as plays, rather than whether they advocated public or private ownership of properties.

The hearings on the Federal Theatre Project ended with Mrs. Flanagan and committee members holding to their conflicting viewpoints. Some critics contended that committee members had set themselves up as censors of the project's plays, in violation of the First Amendment guarantees of freedom of expression.

But in Congress (where Democrats outnumbered Republicans by 76 to 16 in the Senate and 331 to 89 in the House), there were far more defenders of the committee than of the theater project. Various members of both houses, with committee members playing prominent roles, mounted a campaign to abolish the project. They soon succeeded.

The killing of the theater project was regarded by committee members as one of their first major victories. They took the decision as a mandate to launch new and broader investigations.

SOURCES AND SUPPLEMENTARY READING

An article based on the author's interview with the late Representative Martin Dies appeared in the April 29, 1967, issue of *Dawn*, a weekend newspaper supplement.

Excellent accounts of the early days of the House Un-American Activities Committee appear in *The Committee* by Walter Goodman (Farrar, Straus and Giroux, 1968) and *The Un-Americans* by Frank J. Donner.

Throughout the present book, testimony before the Un-American Activities Committee is quoted from committee transcripts and from extracts of those transcripts appearing in *Thirty Years of Treason*, edited by Eric Bentley (Viking Press, 1971). The Bentley book contains useful background material on numerous committee investigations, notably those involving individuals and organizations involved in the arts.

4

★ ★ ★

A Committee under Fire

Congressman Dies, reveling in the publicity and power he had achieved through his chairmanship of HUAC, was determined to keep it in business. Shortly before its term was scheduled to expire, Dies asked the House to extend its life.

Dies held an influential political position at the time. Several public officials who had been severely criticized by his committee had been defeated in the 1938 elections. Moreover, the committee's investigations had won wide support from the public. A Gallup Poll disclosed that almost three-fourths of the people familiar with the work of the committee wanted its investigations continued. Many congressmen were being flooded with mail from constituents, supporting the committee. Thus, despite opposition from members of the Roosevelt administration and some congressional figures, Dies succeeded in winning a one-year extension of the committee's term. The vote in the House favored the extension by 344 to 35. It was the first of several such extensions that were to be granted before the committee eventually was given permanent status.

When Dies requested the extension, he also released the committee's first written report. It accused the Roosevelt administration of failing to pursue alleged subversives with sufficient vigor, and set standards by which the committee planned to define un-American activities. Under these standards, a person would be regarded by the committee as un-American if he believed in: absolute social and racial equality; the idea that it is the "duty of government to support the people"; substitution of communal ownership of property for private ownership; abolition of inheritance; a system of political, economic, or social regimentation based on a planned economy; a collectivist philosophy; or destruction of the American system of checks and balances, with the three independent, coordinate branches of government. Although some of these standards seem extreme today—for example, the one regarding social and racial equality—they were frequently espoused during the late 1930s by Dies and his supporters.

By the time HUAC issued its first report, Dies had installed as the committee's chief investigator a controversial figure named J. B. Matthews. For years, Matthews had been a leader of numerous communist-front organizations. He had spoken frequently and fervently before communist groups and had often written for the Communist Party newspaper, the *Daily Worker*. But by 1938, he had experienced an extreme change of political heart and become a staunch anticommunist. After his conversion, Matthews became a favorite speaker before "patriotic" vigilante groups. It was a short step from that role to his job with the Dies committee, where he served as a sort of professional former communist in residence. He took with him voluminous files on radical organizations —which contained thousands of names of persons who immediately were added to Dies's lists of potential "suspects."

The treatment given Matthews by the committee was typical of the reception accorded some former communists. Those ex-communists who publicly repented, identified their former associates, and became ardent anticommunists could become heroes to the committee and other witch-hunting groups; those who refused to become informers were still regarded as subversives by Dies and his cohorts. In their eyes, a person could prove his conversion from communism only by becoming an outspoken anticommunist.

Late in 1939, Matthews served in the forefront of a Dies committee investigation of an organization he had once headed. The organization, named the American League for Peace and Democracy (ALPD), had formerly been known as the American League Against War and Fascism. Under its former name, its first national chairman had been J. B. Matthews. The league was one of many left-wing organizations—communist and noncommunist—that had banded together in a loose alliance known as the popular front. Although the groups in the popular front often had divergent views on some issues, they managed to combine forces on such other issues as peace, civil rights, and antifascism.

The ALPD had about 20,000 members, including some communists and many noncommunists prominent in government and other fields. The Dies committee, however, set out to try to show that the communists dominated and manipulated the organization. Since many league members were federal officials, Dies saw the investigation as a new opportunity to embarrass the Roosevelt administration. He ignored the fact that some of his fellow members of Congress supported the league and that its work was praised by many of the nation's leading publications.

Committee investigators raided the league's offices in Washington and Chicago, seizing large numbers of documents—including mailing lists. The legality of the seizures was highly questionable and sharply disputed, since no law gives congressional committees power to conduct raids; congressional committees do have the power to issue subpoenas for the production of documents, but the persons issued the subpoenas have the right to challenge them in court. Dies and Matthews, however, showed no hesitation in using the documents in the committee hearings.

The hearings disclosed that such prominent members of the Roosevelt administration as Secretary of the Interior Harold Ickes and Solicitor General Robert H. Jackson (later to be attorney general and a Supreme Court justice) had sent cordial messages to meetings of the league. Dies made public, over objections from more liberal committee members, a list of names found in the league's Washington office. Neither Dies nor anyone else could say whether it was a membership list or a mailing list. Among those on the list were 563 employees of the federal government, including an assistant secretary of the interior, members of the National Labor Relations Board and the Maritime Labor Board, and a high official of the Agricultural Adjustment Administration.

The release of the list caused a furor. Numerous critics

of the committee complained that it was an irresponsible attempt at intimidation. One committee member who had not approved release of the list, Democratic Congressman John Dempsey of New Mexico, charged that it was full of inaccuracies.

Another committee member, who had pressed for release of the list, Republican Congressman Noah Mason of Illinois, defended the committee's action. "If there were mistakes of names being on the list that were not members, it was not the mistake of the Dies committee," Mason claimed. Mason's argument, however, ignored several pertinent facts: the league had no part in the release of the list, it had not wanted the list released, and it had not vouched for the list. Even President Roosevelt condemned the committee's publication of the list as a "sordid procedure."

At the time of the list's publication, the league's continued existence was already in doubt. Communist and noncommunist members, as in many popular-front groups of the time, were sharply divided over the signing of a nonaggression pact by the Soviet Union and Nazi Germany. Harassment of members caused by the Dies committee investigation and the release of the list placed further strains on the organization. These strains were heightened by Dies's demands that the Justice Department prosecute the entire league on some sort of criminal charges. Attorney General Frank Murphy replied that he knew of no laws that had been broken by the league and thus could find no basis for a prosecution. But the threat of prosecution raised by Dies's demands added to the uncertainty of the league's future; within several months, members voted to dissolve the organization.

In 1940, Dies began an investigation aimed at members

of the Communist Party itself. Once again, the emphasis was on lists of names. During the ensuing investigation, Dies several times blatantly disregarded the constitutional rights of the persons being investigated. He ordered committee investigators to conduct a series of raids on Communist Party offices in various eastern cities, seizing all the documents they could find.

In Philadelphia, for example, two committee investigators broke into the local Communist Party office, carried away a truckload of documents and literature, then fled into New Jersey. Communist Party officials immediately went into federal court and complained that their constitutional rights had been violated. U.S. District Court Judge George Welsh, incensed by the audacity of the raid, ordered the investigators arrested. He also directed Dies to make no use of the seized records until the court ruled on a Communist Party request for their return. But Dies smugly informed the judge that his order had come too late—that the documents had already been put into the committee's official record.

Less than a month after the Philadelphia raid, Judge Welsh ruled it had been illegal because it had violated the Fourteenth Amendment's provision that no person shall be deprived of "life, liberty or property without due process of law." The judge's written decision emphasized the necessity for protecting the constitutional rights of communists and members of other unpopular groups. "[The communists are] very much in the minority in our country, but their rights which they claim were violated are rights that are sacred to us all," Welsh wrote.

Dies accused Judge Welsh of protecting "agents of foreign dictators who claim constitutional rights and shirk constitutional duties." Dies added: "If we can't

[32]

obtain legally records of a revolutionary group, records that show seditious activities, then there is no way to defend democracy."

Undaunted, Dies pressed on with his campaign to force Communist Party officials to provide the committee with lists of members' names. The party officials, testifying at committee hearings, repeatedly refused to comply. The party secretary for the District of Columbia, a party official from Pittsburgh, and the head of the Massachusetts Young Communist League declined to name their fellow members. These three party officials and two others were cited for contempt by the Dies committee.

There is an established procedure for prosecution of persons accused of contempt of Congress. First, the appropriate congressional committee cites the defendant for contempt, as the Dies committee had done. Next, the full House or Senate—whichever has supposedly been the victim of the purported contempt—must approve the committee action. The Justice Department then asks a federal grand jury to indict the accused person. If he is indicted, he is entitled to a jury trial and, if convicted, may appeal.

Dies did not have the patience to wait for all those steps to be taken. Instead, in the cases of two of the party officials, he never went to the full House for approval of the committee's contempt citations. He simply went to a United States commissioner (a low-level federal magistrate) and got him to issue warrants for the defendants' arrest. Although Dies had no authority to take such a step, the two party officials were jailed briefly until a federal judge ordered them released. A short time later, the judge ruled that Dies had violated the defendants' constitutional rights. As for the three other party officials cited for contempt, one was found not guilty on the ground that the committee had used unconstitutional methods; a second pleaded no contest and was given a six-month suspended sentence and a $150 fine; and the third was convicted and given a thirty-day suspended sentence and a $250 fine.

As one Communist Party official after another refused to provide the demanded names, the process became increasingly tedious, the press began to lose interest in the hearings, and Dies's enthusiasm waned. He quickly brought the hearings to a close without bothering to press for contempt citations against some of the defiant witnesses.

Later in 1940, Congress passed the Smith Act, which made it a federal crime "to knowingly or willfully advocate, abet, advise, or teach the duty, necessity, desirability, or propriety of overthrowing any government in the United States by force and violence." The law, which also provided for the deportation of aliens found to be "subversive," was to become one of the most controversial pieces of legislation passed in years. Although HUAC had little to do with drafting the law, the political climate created by the committee's various hearings was credited with enabling the legislation to sail through the House by a vote of 382 to 4. Throughout its history, the committee—whose investigations were to help Congress draft any necessary legislation—showed little interest in the lawmaking process. It seemed far more concerned with exposure for exposure's sake.

By 1941, with war raging in Europe and the United States preparing for the possibility that it would soon be drawn into the conflict, the government took various steps to put the country on an emergency footing. Among them was the creation of a system of price and rent controls, administered by a new government agency called the Office of Price Administration (OPA). The controls were opposed by many big businessmen, whose interests had long been championed by Congressman Dies.

When President Roosevelt appointed Leon Henderson to head the OPA, Dies took the House floor and complained that "I wouldn't put Henderson in charge of dog catchers." He charged that Henderson had belonged to at least five organizations dominated by communists. A short time later, Dies wrote a letter to the president in which he claimed that Henderson, four of his key aides, and fifty other OPA employees had long records of membership in communist fronts. Henderson replied that he would "eat on the Treasury steps any communist organization to which I belong."

At first, the administration resisted Dies's demands for the firing of the accused officials. But Dies kept applying pressure. Shortly before the House was to vote on a price-fixing bill, Dies made another speech, in which he complained that the OPA employees he had named were still on the government payroll. Dies issued his most severe attacks against Henderson's chief consultant, Robert A. Brady. He charged that Brady had been a member of the ALPD and had once signed a document praising the Soviet government. In addition, Dies sharply criticized a book Brady had written four years earlier. The book described the capitalist business system as "the most completely amoral and materialistic single-purpose institution the human mind has yet devised." It also predicted a struggle for survival between capitalism and socialism, saying a socialist victory would result in the "extermination" of wealthy, powerful forces representing big business, the military, and the churches. To Dies, those were fighting words. "Here is a man who frankly advocates socialism and the destruction of the church," Dies complained. A short time later, Brady was fired from his government job.

Claiming the Brady discharge as a victory, Dies next set his sights on another government agency, the Federal Communications Commission (FCC), which regulates the broadcast industry. His chief target was a former Columbia University professor named Goodwin Watson, who had recently been hired by the FCC as a broadcast analyst. Watson was highly regarded in academic circles as a social psychologist. But Dies, without conducting any committee investigation, complained to FCC Chairman James Fly that Watson was a propagandist for communism. Fly ignored the complaint, and Dies charged Watson with membership in at least thirteen communist-front organizations.

The dispute became more heated when a magazine reported that Dies was the subject of frequent praise in propaganda broadcasts by the Axis powers—Germany, Italy and Japan. The FCC's duties included monitoring such broadcasts. When Dies asked the FCC for an explanation of the magazine report, Chairman Fly replied that Dies had been the subject of as many "favorable references in Axis propaganda as any living American public figure." In retaliation, Dies persuaded his House colleagues to pass an amendment to the FCC appropriation bill that eliminated Professor Watson's salary. The Senate refused to approve the amendment, so Watson remained on the payroll.

Next, Dies launched an attack on Malcolm Cowley, a distinguished literary critic who had joined the government as chief information analyst of the U.S. Office of Facts and Figures, an agency designed to inform Americans about the nation's defense program. Dies claimed that the committee's files showed Cowley to be affiliated with more than seventy communist fronts. Despite his prominence in the literary world, Cowley received little support from government officials in defending himself against Dies's allegations. Two months after Dies first criticized him, Cowley resigned his government job.

After the Japanese attack on Pearl Harbor on December 7, 1941, and the entry of the United States into World War II, Dies briefly concentrated on what he described as Japanese espionage activities within this country. But before long, he was back on the trail of alleged communists and their sympathizers. By that time, the Nazi-Soviet pact had been broken and the Russians had become wartime allies of the Americans. Notwithstanding that alliance, Dies seemed to see greater dangers to the nation's internal security from the communists than from the Nazis or Japanese.

One of Dies's first targets after the United States entered the war was a new government agency called the Board of Economic Warfare (BEW). The agency, headed by Vice-President Henry A. Wallace, had enormous powers concerning accumulation of strategic materials, import-export policy, American investments abroad, the communications industry, shipping, and patents. Wallace, who in past years had denounced the "violence and brutality" of the communist government in Russia, had more recently been increasingly tolerant of communist views at home and abroad. Many of his associates were left-wingers—if not communists then at least "fellow travelers" of the communists.

Congressman Dies released to the press copies of an open letter to Wallace, accusing thirty-five officials of the BEW of belonging to communist-front organizations; most were charged with having belonged to the ALPD. Dies demanded that all the accused officials resign or be fired.

He directed much of his fire at a BEW economist named Maurice Parmalee—not so much because of Parmalee's political affiliations but because he had once written a book, *Nudism in Modern Life*. The book had been ruled obscene by a federal judge, but that decision had been overturned by an appeals court. Still, the idea of the BEW's employing an author whose book had contained photographs of nudes was too much for Dies. "There is no place in such an agency for an outstanding advocate of nudism," he said.

Vice-President Wallace accused Dies of publicity-seeking, pointing out that the committee chairman had not called the charges to his attention before releasing them to the press. It later developed that Dies had not even discussed the matter with fellow members of his committee. Increasingly, he was inclined to act as a one-man committee. Wallace, despite his distaste for Dies's techniques, asked the FBI to investigate the backgrounds of the thirty-five accused officials.

In due course, the FBI reported that it could find no evidence of disloyalty among any of them. Nonetheless, the embattled Parmalee was fired—with the BEW claiming that a reorganization of the agency had eliminated the need for his job. Meanwhile, another of the thirty-five BEW officials, David B. Vaughn, filed a $750,000 lawsuit against Dies, contending that he had been falsely accused of subversive activities. An investigation later disclosed that another man named David B. Vaughn, who was not a government employee, had once belonged to the ALPD. Dies and his researchers had never bothered to check on his identity. Dies publicly apologized to Vaughn, withdrew the charges, and offered to pay Vaughn's legal fees if the lawsuit were dropped. Vaughn agreed. The legal fees, totaling more than $600, were not paid personally by Dies but by the House of Representatives.

If Dies was embarrassed by the case of mistaken identity or the fact that the FBI had cleared all thirty-five BEW officials, he showed no sign of it. Early in 1941, Congress had appropriated $100,000 for an investigation by the Justice Department of government workers suspected of membership in subversive organizations. In October, Dies sent Attorney General Francis Biddle a list of 1,121 federal employees he accused of subversive activities. He demanded they be fired, claiming their government employment provided evidence that "there is a new influx of subversive elements into official Washington."

After investigating all 1,121 persons, the Justice Department found reason for the firing of only two. Attorney General Biddle said most of the names had merely been taken from mailing lists of left-wing organizations, and he denied there were grounds for broad accusations of subversion among government employees.

Dies, infuriated, took the House floor and charged Biddle with failing to carry out properly the duties given him by Congress. The substance of his speech was that the Justice Department should have taken his word, and forced them off the federal payroll. Biddle replied that he had no intention of allowing the department to become a rubber stamp for Dies.

Dies released still another list of federal employees. He did not even claim that they were communists or disloyal to the government, but simply that they were "radical and crackpot." And he warned the administration that, if it failed to dismiss the employees, Congress would refuse to appropriate money to pay their salaries.

Several days later, an appropriation bill covering the Treasury Department was called up for consideration by the House. An ally of Dies, Democratic Congressman Joe Hendricks of Florida, proposed an amendment to the bill that would forbid use of any part of the appropriation to pay the salary of anyone on Dies's latest list. Actually, only one of the thirty-nine named—an economist, William Pickens—worked for the Treasury Department. But since all government checks were drawn against the U.S. Treasury, Hendricks contended that the appropriate way to cut off paychecks to all thirty-nine was by amending the treasury appropriation bill. If his fellow House members were unwilling to accept that interpretation, he said, he was prepared to tack similar amendments onto future appropriation bills covering other agencies.

Many House members—including some who had usually supported the Dies committee—were indeed unwilling to accept Hendricks's interpretation, and his proposed amendment was defeated by the House. He then filed a new amendment providing for the abolition of only Pickens's salary, making no reference to the other thirty-eight employees. The second amendment was passed by the House.

A new uproar was touched off by the action against Pickens. Treasury Department officials issued a statement contending they had previously studied the allegations against him and found that "Mr. Pickens is completely loyal to the government of the United States." Pickens, before taking his government job, had been a dean at several Negro colleges and an official of the National

[40]

Association for the Advancement of Colored People (NAACP). At the Treasury Department, his work involved promoting the sale of government savings bonds among Negro organizations.

It was not until after the House had voted to cut off Pickens's salary that many of the members learned he was a Negro. Belatedly, they realized that they might be criticized on the ground that they had singled him out because of his race, rather than because he was the only Treasury Department employee on Dies's list. Congressmen who supported the Roosevelt administration introduced a measure to overturn the amendment cutting off Pickens's salary and to substitute for it a resolution giving a House appropriations subcommittee the power to investigate all charges of subversive activities by government employees. The resolution, it seemed clear, would undercut the authority of the Dies committee.

It prompted spirited debate, both on the question of Pickens's race and on the threat it posed to HUAC. Democratic Congressman John Rankin of Mississippi, a Dies supporter and an outspoken advocate of white supremacy, argued: "I voted to strike him [Pickens] off when I thought he was a white man and I shall certainly not vote to put him back on because he is a Negro." Rankin's fellow Mississippian, Democrat W. M. Colmer, charged: "Somebody is playing to the Negro vote." But other congressmen contended that the elimination of Pickens's salary, if it did not constitute actual racism, at least gave the appearance of racism. One said the action verged on "lynch law."

The House passed the new resolution giving investigative powers to the appropriations subcommittee on February 9, 1943, and reversed the action barring salary

[41]

payments to Pickens. Congressman John Kerr, a North Carolina Democrat, was appointed chairman. Dies said he would make available to Kerr information from his files on the thirty-nine persons included on his latest list, and on many other government employees.

Some critics charged that the Kerr committee quickly became almost as unfair to those it was investigating as the Dies committee had been. The new panel conducted its hearings behind closed doors, barred those under investigation from bringing lawyers with them, and refused to allow them to cross-examine witnesses. For its initial investigations, the Kerr committee chose six persons from Dies's list of thirty-nine. One of the six was Goodwin Watson, the FCC broadcast analyst previously accused by Dies of serving as a propagandist for communism. Two others were also FCC employees, Frederick Schuman and William Dodd. The three others, all employed by the Interior Department, were Robert M. Lovett, Arthur Goldschmidt, and Jack Fahy.

All six were summoned to testify before the Kerr committee, where they were questioned about their political beliefs and about organizations to which they reportedly belonged. At the conclusion of the hearings, the committee announced that it was taking no action against Schuman, Goldschmidt, and Fahy because of lack of sufficient evidence. But it declared Watson, Dodd, and Lovett "unfit to continue in government employment." The committee did not accuse the "unfit" three of being communists or of improperly carrying out their government duties. Rather, it charged that they should be disqualified from federal service because they had been active in organizations designated as subversive by the

attorney general or because they had criticized the capitalist system and specific government policies.

The full House Appropriations Committee approved
the findings of the Kerr panel and voted to amend an
appropriations bill to provide for the elimination of the
salaries of Watson, Dodd, and Lovett. When the measure
went to the Senate, the amendment was defeated in four
separate votes. The appropriations bill, which was badly
needed to pay the salaries of thousands of federal employees, was stalemated because of the failure of the
House and Senate to agree. Finally, the two houses
reached a compromise providing that President Roosevelt would have to reappoint Watson, Dodd, and Lovett
and get the appointments confirmed by the Senate within
six months in order for them to keep their jobs. The
Senate agreed on the compromise grudgingly, with many
senators explaining they had voted for it only because
of the urgent necessity for passing the appropriations bill.

Several troublesome questions were posed by the
compromise. One involved the relationship between the
executive and legislative branches of government. Critics
of the compromise argued that Congress had no right to
dictate to the Roosevelt administration on who might or
might not be given a job in the executive branch. But
supporters of the Kerr committee replied that, since
Congress controlled the government purse strings, it was
the employer of all federal office-holders and had the
right to determine their fitness for employment.

Another troublesome question raised by the compromise was the issue of whether the congressional action
against Watson, Dodd, and Lovett amounted to an illegal
bill of attainder. Bills of attainder, legislative acts that
provide punishment without giving their victims the

[43]

benefit of criminal trials, are specifically prohibited by the U.S. Constitution.

President Roosevelt denounced the compromise as an unconstitutional "encroachment" on the powers of the executive branch. He said he would have vetoed the appropriations bill containing the compromise amendment except for the fact that the money provided by the measure was desperately needed to keep the government operating during wartime. Instead, he signed the bill but said that he did not consider the compromise amendment binding on the executive branch. Accordingly, he did not reappoint Watson, Dodd, and Lovett and then ask for Senate confirmation—as required by the amendment. He simply retained them in their jobs, without pay, after the six-month deadline set by Congress. Meanwhile, the three officials, with the help of Justice Department lawyers, filed a lawsuit testing the validity of the amendment and demanding that their salaries be paid.

A federal court decided the case in their favor. The case was appealed to the Supreme Court, which eventually upheld the lower-court ruling in a unanimous decision in June 1946. The language employed by Justice Hugo Black, who wrote the Supreme Court decision, bore a significance that went beyond the case at hand and applied to many other attempts by congressional committees to oust federal employees because of their beliefs or associations.

As a result of the Supreme Court decision, neither the Dies committee nor any other congressional committee tried again to punish individuals it disliked by pushing through legislation to cut off their salaries. However, many other techniques of punishment remained available to congressmen. There was, for example, the simple means of rising on the floor of Congress and accusing a person of all manner of heinous acts—knowing that no proof would be required and that no slander or libel suits could result from statements made before Congress or any of its committees. There was also the technique of calling a friendly witness before a congressional committee and allowing him to blacken the name of anyone he chose. A more subtle method involved insertion of derogatory material about an individual into the records of a congressional committee, without giving the person a chance to defend himself. A congressman could then "leak" information about the accused person to the press, emphasizing that the derogatory material came straight from the committee files. The fact that it was in the files, of course, did not make it true. But the press often would fail to make that distinction, leading the public to believe that, since the information came from the "official" files, it must be accurate.

Martin Dies and his committee colleagues used all these techniques, and others, both before and after the Supreme Court decision in the case of Watson, Dodd, and Lovett. In early 1944, with President Roosevelt preparing to run for reelection to a fourth term, Dies sought new ways to embarrass the administration. He centered his attack on the president's ties with the labor movement.

One of Roosevelt's closest advisers was Sidney Hillman, chairman of the CIO Political Action Committee (PAC) —the chief political voice of organized labor. Dies and his supporters had been stung by the fact that the PAC, with its large budget and strong influence on the votes of union members, had been campaigning for the defeat at the polls of most members of HUAC. Since the committee claimed to be protecting the government against communism, Dies concluded that the PAC's opposition to committee members was evidence that the PAC was pro-communist. This sort of logic was not peculiar to Dies alone; it would be adopted by several future chairmen and members of HUAC. By their simplistic standards, those who supported the committee were obviously anti-communists and those who opposed the committee were just as obviously procommunists.

In a speech on the House floor, Dies charged that Hillman would soon become "head of the communists in the United States." He issued subpoenas calling for Hill-man to testify before the committee and to produce the PAC's financial records. Hillman refused to turn over the records, arguing that the Dies committee had no jurisdiction to investigate a political organization. (He did, however, agree to deliver the records to both the FBI and a congressional committee on campaign expenditures.) Dies, unable to get his hands on the records, did not even call Hillman to testify.

The committee staff, without calling witnesses, carried out a perfunctory investigation of the PAC. It put together a list of telegrams and telephone calls between officials of the PAC and the Roosevelt regime, purporting to show that the PAC was the "political arm" of the administration. Dies, acting as if association with the PAC were a criminal offense, demanded that the Justice Department prosecute more than seventy administration officials he accused of improper connections with the organization. The Justice Department ignored him.

For many proadministration House members, the report on the PAC represented what they considered the latest in a long line of irresponsible investigative actions. The committee was still operating on a temporary year-to-year basis and its opponents reasoned that when Congress opened its new term in January 1945 they could muster the votes to kill any proposal to continue the committee's operations. Martin Dies, who was in poor health, had announced earlier in the year that he would not seek reelection. With Dies no longer in the House, they figured, support for the committee would be greatly diminished.

But they were in for a surprise. They had neglected to take into account the shrewdness and parliamentary skills of one of the committee's most ardent backers—a Mississippi Democratic congressman named John Rankin.

SOURCES AND SUPPLEMENTARY READING

Walter Goodman's *The Committee*, Frank Donner's *The Un-Americans*, and Telford Taylor's *Grand Inquest* all provide valuable material about this period.

It should be noted that these books have differing strengths and weaknesses. *The Committee*, while the most exhaustive, seems to waver at times between condemnation of the witch-hunt philosophy of the Un-American Activities Committee and distaste for the beliefs and activities of the witch-hunt victims. *The Un-Americans* suffers from a shrill tone perhaps attributable to the fact that the author himself was a victim of the witch hunters. Still, it documents numerous case histories worth examination. *Grand Inquest*, written by a respected attorney who served as a chief prosecutor of Nazi war criminals after World War II, is lucid, fair, and authoritative but may occasionally seem ponderous.

5
★ ★ ★

Permanent Status
for the Committee

To many politically aware Americans, John Rankin's most obvious attribute was his blatant racism. The Mississippi congressman made no secret of his hatred for blacks, Jews, and other minority groups.

There was a tendency in some quarters to dismiss Rankin as the prototype of the demagogic southern politician—supposedly lacking in intelligence and succeeding merely by catering to the prejudices of his constituents. But that assessment sold him short, for, along with his demagoguery and bigotry, Rankin possessed a keen mind and an extensive knowledge of the intricacies of congressional procedure.

He immediately put his parliamentary skills to work on behalf of HUAC when the new Congress convened in 1945. Theoretically, the existence of all congressional committees and the authority of all congressional rules end at the conclusion of each term of Congress. Therefore, the first orders of business at each new session normally include adopting the rules of the previous Congress and reestablishing all permanent committees. The procedures are usually mere formalities. But in 1945, Rankin contrived to make them far more than that.

Rankin knew that the congressmen bent on killing the special investigating committee were depending on the routine formalities. Once those steps were accomplished, they planned to refer to the powerful Rules Committee any proposal to extend the life of the temporary Un-American Activities Committee. The Rules Committee, headed by Democratic Congressman Adolph Sabath of Illinois, would be dominated by proadministration members who could be expected to conduct lengthy hearings on the issue and eventually vote against extending the term.

In a move that took other House members completely by surprise, Rankin executed a parliamentary maneuver designed to get around the established procedures. When the supposedly routine motion was made to adopt the rules of the previous Congress, Rankin offered a proposed amendment to the rules which provided for making the Un-American Activities Committee permanent, with broad investigative powers. Since the House had not yet voted to reestablish the Rules Committee or any of its other committees, it could not refer Rankin's proposal to the Rules Committee. Therefore, the matter would have to be decided by the entire House.

Rankin's surprise tactic caught critics of HUAC napping. They had confidently expected to see the committee's existence ended, but, until Rankin's proposed amendment was decided upon, the House could not get on with the business of organizing itself for the new session.

Knowing he had many congressmen in an uncomfortable

spot, Rankin pressed his advantage. The Un-American Activities Committee, although despised by large numbers of congressmen, had an enthusiastic following among the citizenry and numerous self-described patriotic organizations, including the American Legion. He knew that few congressmen, no matter what their positions on the committee, would want to offend a group with such powerful influence as the Legion. Rankin implied that it would be unpatriotic to vote against his amendment.

Opposition to the amendment was led by House Majority Leader John McCormack of Massachusetts, who pointed out that passage of Rankin's proposal would break a long-standing tradition in Congress: the practice was to appoint a temporary committee to conduct an investigation on a given subject within a specified time limit.

Rankin replied that the Un-American Activities Committee would not be substantially different from any other committee of the House—in addition to carrying out investigations, it would conduct hearings on proposed legislation. But he was unable to say what sort of legislation the committee might consider. Other congressional committees held clearly defined jurisdictions over such subjects as foreign affairs, military policy, taxation, and agriculture. The subject of "un-American activities"— a term that was not defined in Rankin's amendment— did not seem to lend itself to clear jurisdiction. And McCormack pointed out that the Un-American Activities Committee's attempts to oversee legislation might invade the jurisdictions of other committees.

McCormack's argument was one that was to be heard many times over the years in relation to the Un-American Activities Committee, but Rankin never even tried to answer the question about the type of legislation to be considered by the committee.

Rankin's argument was that the abolition of the committee would lead to destruction of the extensive files collected by Martin Dies and J. B. Matthews. He claimed the attempt to kill the committee was part of a subversive plot to get rid of the files and thus hide the "sins" of the country's enemies: ". . . these valuable records that probably involve the fate of the nation, the safety of the American people, would be dissipated. I want to see that these papers are kept."

Actually, steps had already been taken to assure that the files—whatever their merits—would be preserved even if the committee were abolished. But Rankin claimed that such action was merely a smoke screen to help conceal the supposed plot aimed at the files' destruction.

When the House first voted on Rankin's amendment, it was by a voice vote, in which no record was made of how each member cast his ballot. The vote was 146 to 134 against the amendment. But Rankin was not finished. Knowing that many congressmen would be reluctant to go on record as voting against the committee, in view of its popularity among many citizens, Rankin insisted on a roll-call vote on his amendment. That vote resulted in passage of the amendment, 207 to 186. Rankin, elated with his victory, gloated: "I caught 'em flat-footed and flat-headed."

By such odd circumstances was the committee saved from extinction and granted permanent status. As sponsor of the amendment giving the committee that status, Rankin ordinarily would have been in line to succeed Dies as chairman. But he was already chairman of the Veterans Affairs Committee, and House rules prohibited any mem-

[51]

ber from heading more than one permanent committee. With World War II nearing an end, Rankin anticipated the Veterans Affairs Committee would soon assume increasing importance and he thus declined to resign his chairmanship. As a result, the nominal chairmanship was given to Democratic Congressman Edward J. Hart of New Jersey. But Rankin became the most powerful member of the committee, dictating its policy and controlling its staff. Other members of the committee as it resumed work were Democrats J. W. Robinson of Utah, J. Hardin Peterson of Florida, Herbert Bonner of North Carolina, and John Murdock of Arizona; and Republicans J. Parnell Thomas of New Jersey and Karl Mundt of South Dakota.

On April 12, 1945, President Roosevelt died and was succeeded in office by Vice-President Truman. Since Truman made clear that he intended to carry out many of Roosevelt's New Deal policies, he inherited from his predecessor the antagonism of members of the HUAC. Shortly after Truman entered the White House, the committee launched a new investigation of the Office of Price Administration. Rankin, like Dies, had close ties with big businessmen who viewed the OPA's control over prices and rents as a dangerous step toward socialism. Echoing this view, Rankin referred to OPA officials as "commissars" and announced his intention to try to abolish the agency.

The investigation was directed chiefly against a weekly radio program, "Soldiers with Coupons," which was produced by the OPA. (The title stemmed from the fact that the OPA, among its other duties, issued ration coupons to consumers entitling them to buy products that were subject to wartime shortages. Depending on a family's size and needs, it would receive a certain number of

[52]

coupons for purchase of such items as sugar, butter, and gasoline. Customers were required by law to present the coupons when making their purchases.) The radio programs frequently contained dramatizations in which customers were pictured as being victimized by greedy businessmen and landlords. They emphasized that the OPA was designed to protect the "little man" against such abuses. But neither Rankin nor anyone else was able to provide proof of specific subversive activities within the agency. The investigation quickly petered out without posing more than a vague threat to the OPA's continued existence.

In July 1945, the committee began the first of several investigations it would eventually conduct into alleged subversion in the motion-picture industry. Committee investigators were sent to Hollywood to investigate what Rankin called "one of the most dangerous plots ever instigated for the overthrow of the government." The decision to launch the investigation was made at a committee meeting at which Chairman Hart was not present; he considered this an affront to his dignity, and promptly resigned—giving ill health as the excuse. Democratic Congressman John Wood of Georgia replaced him as the committee's nominal chairman.

The Hollywood investigation continued, with Rankin promising that it would expose persons "insidiously trying to spread subversive propaganda, poison the minds of your children, distort the history of our country and discredit Christianity." But these persons were never identified. Despite Rankin's promises, no revelations were produced. After reaping a harvest of newspaper headlines with its unsubstantiated charges, the committee moved on to an investigation of the broadcasting industry.

[53]

Rankin had installed as chief counsel to the committee a politically conservative lawyer from Georgia named Ernie Adamson. Without seeking approval from the full committee, Adamson asked seven New York radio news commentators to submit batches of their scripts for examination. By Adamson's standards, the commentators were suspect on various grounds—among them, that they had exhibited the audacity to criticize members of Congress or that some of them had been born abroad. When some members of Congress complained that the request for the scripts posed a threat to freedom of the press and others pointed out that the full committee had not authorized Adamson's action, Rankin jumped to his defense: "Some of those scripts ought not to be drummed into the ears of the American people." Two of the seven commentators, without being given any sort of hearings, were dismissed by their radio stations.

Committee Chairman Wood introduced a bill that would have required all radio commentators to register their places of birth, nationalities, and political affiliations for inspection by the public. The proposal drew new objections that the committee was trying to stifle freedom of speech and of the press. A group calling itself Citizens to Abolish the Wood-Rankin Committee took an advertisement in the *New York Times* headlined: "You Can't Talk—It's Un-American." The committee promptly began an investigation of the group. Wood's bill never got off the ground, and the investigation of the broadcasting industry proved as unproductive in exposing subversion as the Hollywood investigation.

After World War II ended in the late summer of 1945, the committee opened new investigations of the Communist Party and its alleged front groups. Among the most prominent of the groups was the Joint Anti-Fascist Refugee Committee, which provided medical services and other aid to refugees who had fled to France during the Spanish Civil War. The refugee committee was staunchly opposed to the Spanish government of dictator Francisco Franco, whose rebel troops had won the civil war against loyalist forces backed by the communists. Congressmen Rankin and Wood supported Franco's regime and regarded opposition to his government as evidence of un-Americanism. They charged that the refugee committee's attacks on Franco represented distribution of propaganda of "a subversive character."

The committee subpoenaed sixteen officials of the organization and the executive secretary, and ordered them to surrender their membership records and other files. The officials refused to do so on various grounds. The committee voted to cite the seventeen members of the organization for contempt of Congress. All the defendants were tried in federal court and convicted. Those who were sentenced to jail appealed their convictions on the grounds that the subpoenas for their files had been invalid and that the committee had exceeded its jurisdiction.

The appeal was heard by three judges of the U.S. Court of Appeals for the District of Columbia. One judge voted to reverse the convictions, writing an opinion that sharply criticized the committee. "In my opinion the House committee investigation abridges freedom of speech and inflicts punishment without trial," he said. But he was outvoted by the other two judges, who ruled that it was the business of Congress, not the courts, to deal with any improper conduct that might be practiced by a congressional committee. The Supreme Court declined to take up the case, and the defendants who had been given jail terms were forced to serve their sentences.

In the November 1946 elections, the Republicans won control of both houses. They thus gained the right to take over the chairmanships of all committees, plus voting majorities on the committees, and power to name most staff members when the new Congress convened in January 1947. The Democrats on the Un-American Activities Committee, knowing they would soon have to surrender control, used the waning days of 1946 to make a variety of unsubstantiated charges and conduct hearings destined to capture the spotlight of national publicity.

The hearings centered on the testimony of a former communist named Louis Budenz, who was to become one of the most famous professional witnesses in the anticommunist movement. While a Communist Party member, Budenz had been an editor of the party's newspaper, the *Daily Worker*, and understood very well the workings of the news media. Once he broke with communism in 1945, he capitalized on that knowledge to gain a maximum of publicity for his charges of subversive activities by others.

In late 1946, Budenz made a radio speech in which he charged that a mysterious Soviet agent was giving orders to communists throughout the United States. He provided a dramatic description of the supposed agent's operations, claiming the man communicated his directives to communists without ever meeting them face to face: "Communist leaders never see him, but they follow his orders or suggestions implicitly." He did not identify the purported agent in his speech, which received wide press coverage. Two days later, HUAC, apparently sensing a publicity bonanza, announced that it was calling Budenz as a witness.

Before appearing at the committee hearing, Budenz publicly identified the man he claimed was the Soviet agent. He named Gerhart Eisler, who had been born in Austria and had later lived in Germany before entering the United States in 1941. While living in New York during the next five years, Eisler had retained his German citizenship. He and his wife had been scheduled to return to Germany on the day after he was identified by Budenz. But on the basis of Budenz's charges, U.S. immigration authorities canceled their permits.

When Budenz appeared at the hearing, he spoke at length about his own membership in the Communist Party and his reasons for leaving it. But when it came to testifying about Eisler, he could provide no proof to support his charges. Although Eisler was in the audience during Budenz's testimony, the committee did not immediately give him a chance to rebut the charges.

It was not until two months later, on February 6, 1947, that Eisler was called before the committee. By that time, the new Congress had been seated and the Republicans had taken control of the committee. The new chairman was J. Parnell Thomas, the Republican from New Jersey who had been a member of the committee since its formation. Thomas was as zealous in his hunt for alleged subversives as his predecessors in the chairmanship. He considered the New Deal policies subversive and was determined to drive from the Truman administration every possible official who had been involved in devising them.

Democratic Congressmen Rankin, Wood, Peterson, and Bonner remained on the committee when the new term began, as did Republican Representative Mundt. There were three new Republican members—John McDowell of Pennsylvania, Richard Vail of Illinois, and a freshman

congressman from California named Richard Nixon—
who was later to play a prominent role in the committee.
The Republicans fired Ernie Adamson as the committee's
chief counsel and replaced him with Robert Stripling,
who had begun working for the committee as an investigator during Martin Dies's chairmanship.

Between the time of Budenz's testimony about him and
his own appearance before the committee, Eisler had been
taken into custody by U.S. immigration officers and held
as an illegal alien in a cell on Ellis Island in New York
harbor. Before being sworn in as a witness by the committee, Eisler insisted on being allowed to read a statement
in which he would claim he was a "political prisoner."
Chairman Thomas refused to permit this, ruling that the
witness would be allowed to deliver prepared remarks only
after answering the committee's questions. The dispute
was not so trivial as it seemed. On various occasions,
the chairmen of HUAC had promised to permit such prepared statements at the conclusion of witnesses' testimony
—only to renege if displeased by the testimony. Under
this stipulation, Eisler refused to be sworn in, and was
cited for contempt.

With that, Eisler was taken from the witness chair by
immigration officers and escorted back to his cell on
Ellis Island. Other witnesses, including Eisler's sister (with
whom he was not on speakng terms), later testified that
he had been involved in numerous communist activities.
There seemed little doubt that Eisler was indeed active
in various communist circles, but the committee never
produced evidence sufficient to sustain Budenz's sensational allegations—which had been given wide distribution
with the encouragement of the committee.

Congressman Nixon, in his first speech on the House

[58]

floor, asked for approval of the committee's action in citing Eisler for contempt. Nixon's speech included several unproved allegations against Eisler and several others that seemed to have no basis in fact. But the House, with only one member voting "no," approved the resolution citing Eisler for contempt.

Eisler was convicted in federal court and sentenced to a year in prison and a $1,000 fine. While his attorneys appealed the case, he was released on bail. Left-wing groups sponsored numerous rallies around the country in support of Eisler, who claimed to be the victim of "a witch-hunting hysteria in this country." Later, while his appeal was being considered by the Supreme Court, Eisler jumped his bail and stowed away aboard a Polish ship headed from New York to England. He was arrested when the ship reached England, but a London judge refused to extradite him to the United States and allowed him to proceed to communist East Germany. Eisler never returned to the United States. He died in 1968 in the Armenian Soviet Republic, where he had gone to help negotiate a contract between the East German and Russian radio networks.

In addition to investigating Eisler in 1947, the committee launched a broad range of other activities. All were designed to implement a newly adopted eight-point program:

1. To expose and ferret out the communists and communist sympathizers in the federal government.

2. To spotlight the spectacle of having outright communists controlling and dominating some of the most vital unions in American labor.

3. To institute a counter-educational program

against the subversive propaganda which has been hurled at the American people.

4. Investigation of those groups and movements which are trying to dissipate our atomic-bomb knowledge for the benefit of a foreign power.

5. Investigation of communist influences in Hollywood.

6. Investigation of communist influences in education.

7. Organization of the research staff so as to furnish reference service to members of Congress and to keep them currently informed on all subjects relating to subversive and un-American activities in the United States.

8. Continued accumulation of files and records to be placed at the disposal of the investigative units of the government and armed services.

Meanwhile, President Truman—in a move the committee claimed credit for precipitating—acted to put the executive branch of government more directly in the business of purging its ranks of suspected subversives. The president issued an executive order directing the establishment of a complex loyalty-review system throughout the government. Each department of the executive branch created its own loyalty board, whose members were named by the department head. An employee or prospective employee of a department who was suspected of subversive activities or sympathies would first be investigated by the departmental loyalty board. The board would then make recommendations on the case to the department head, who could accept or reject them. If the employee was dissatisfied with the outcome—for example, if he was fired or suspended from his job—he could appeal the decision.

Permanent civil service employees were given the right of direct appeal to a twenty-three-member Loyalty Review Board appointed by the president. Temporary employees could appeal to regional loyalty boards established in each section of the country. If dissatisfied with those appeals, they could then take their cases to the national board.

On the surface, the loyalty-review system seemed designed to provide a relatively fair method of protecting the employees' rights. But in practice, the system was subject to numerous abuses, and the loyalty-review boards sometimes became vehicles for political witch hunts. To begin with, the system did not require proof of an employee's membership in an organization deemed subversive. He could be fired merely for "sympathetic association" with an unpopular political movement or with "a group or combination of persons" regarded as subversive. Such vague terms obviously were subject to numerous interpretations and thus to possible abuses. Moreover, the means of determining which organizations and movements were to be regarded as subversive left much to be desired. The attorney general was directed to compile lists of organizations that were to be considered off-limits for government employees. The attorney general, in turn, was to rely heavily on such sources as the files of HUAC and the FBI—which in many cases were highly suspect.

In some quarters, a virtual obsession developed about the making of lists. Thousands of self-described "patriots" began compiling their own lists of supposed subversives. Countless tracts were circulated throughout the country, assailing certain individuals on the grounds of their "associations." The facts in each case tended to be obscured. (The obsession with list-making apparently persists in some quarters today. In 1973, it was disclosed that aides of President Richard Nixon had prepared lists of political enemies who might be subjected to reprisals such as harassment by the Internal Revenue Service.)

The loyalty program was eventually recognized by Truman himself as subject to various failings: once a person had been cleared, all of the data remained in the review board files; with each job change, the file was reviewed and the individual had to answer the same charges again and again. Truman later wrote in his memoirs that it was "not in the tradition of American fair play and justice."

HUAC was caught in a peculiar position by Truman's Loyalty Order. On the one hand, committee members claimed it was their pressure and their "revelations" that had forced the president to act. On the other hand, some of them were dismayed by the realization that Truman's action might take the play away from them on the antisubversive front—depriving them of the publicity that had been the committee's lifeblood.

To take the initiative back from Truman and place the committee once again in the limelight, Chairman Thomas and his colleagues decided to launch another sensational investigation by reopening the question of alleged subversion in Hollywood. What could be more fascinating to Americans, the committee reasoned, than allegations against some of the biggest names in the nation's most glamorous business?

SOURCES AND SUPPLEMENTARY READING

Harry S Truman's *Memoirs* (Doubleday, 1955 and 1956) describes the former president's continuing struggle against the Un-American Activities Committee and other witch-hunting organizations.

Additional Dialogue (Bantam, 1972), a collection of letters written by blacklisted screen writer Dalton Trumbo (whose confrontations with the Un-American Activities Committee will be described later), provides fascinating glimpses into the world of witch-hunt victims in the entertainment business.

Eric Bentley's *Thirty Years of Treason* contains not only extracts of testimony but also relevant background information on the committee's investigations of members of the Eisler family.

6
★ ★ ★
The Witch Hunters
Strike Hollywood

The entire premise of the Hollywood investigation was that subversives throughout the motion-picture industry were flooding the country with films contrived to peddle communist propaganda. In a series of hearings that stretched over nine years, the committee was never able to substantiate such charges, but the hearings did produce vast amounts of publicity and some evidence of communist activity in Hollywood.

The hearings opened in Washington on October 20, 1947, in a committee room jammed with newsmen. The initial witnesses, considered friendly to the committee, were permitted to make damaging charges against Hollywood figures without providing any substantiating evidence. Mrs. Lela Rogers, the mother of actress Ginger Rogers, cited as evidence of communist infiltration of Hollywood the fact that the original script of the film *Tender Comrade* had called upon her daughter to speak the line: "Share and share alike—that's democracy." Mrs. Rogers said that her

[64]

daughter had refused to utter the line, and that it had been cut from the script. She testified that she had prevented her daughter from appearing in movies that gave a depressing view of life in the United States, since she felt such films served the purposes of the communists.

Among the most cooperative of the friendly witnesses was character actor Adolphe Menjou, who had worked in the motion-picture industry for thirty-four years. Menjou described himself as a student of the dangers of communism and testified about what he regarded as subversive influences in Hollywood.

Menjou was followed to the witness chair by Robert Taylor, one of Hollywood's most popular leading men of the period. Taylor did not pretend to be nearly so knowledgeable as Menjou about communism, but he received an equally warm reception from the committee. The committee room was crowded with female movie-goers anxious for close-up looks at the handsome film star. The questioning followed a similar pattern, and Committee Counsel Robert Stripling was particularly interested in the Screen Actors Guild:

STRIPLING: Are you a member of any guild?

TAYLOR: I am a member of the Screen Actors Guild; yes, sir.

STRIPLING: Have you ever noticed any elements within the Screen Actors Guild that you would consider to be following the Communist Party line?

TAYLOR: Well, yes, sir, I must confess that I have. . . . Quite recently I have been very active as a director of that board. It seems to me that at meetings, especially meetings of the general membership of the guild, there is always a certain group of actors

[65]

and actresses whose every action would indicate to me that, if they are not communists, they are working awfully hard to be communists. I don't know. Their tactics and their philosophies seem to me to be pretty much Party-line stuff.

STRIPLING: Mr. Taylor, these people in the Screen Actors Guild who, in your opinion, follow the Communist Party line, are they a disrupting influence within the organization?

TAYLOR: It seems so to me.

STRIPLING: Do you recall the names of any of the actors in the guild who participated in such activity?

TAYLOR: Well, yes, sir, I can name a few who seem to sort of disrupt things once in a while. Whether or not they are communists I don't know.

STRIPLING: Would you name them for the committee, please?

TAYLOR: One chap we have currently, I think, is Mr. Howard Da Silva. He always seems to have something to say at the wrong time. Miss Karen Morley also usually appears at the guild meetings. . . . Those are two I can think of right at the moment. . . .

The day after Taylor's testimony, the committee called as a witness actor Ronald Reagan, who was then president of the Screen Actors Guild and was later elected governor of California. Stripling asked him whether he had ever encountered an attempt by communists to exert influence within the guild. Reagan replied:

There has been a small group within the Screen Actors Guild which has consistently opposed the policy of the guild board and officers of the guild, as

[66]

evidenced by the vote on various issues. That small clique referred to has been suspected of more or less following the tactics that we associate with the Communist Party.

The next witness was one of the most popular stars in Hollywood history, Gary Cooper. He had acquired an enormous following through his appearances in such films as *Unconquered, Pride of the Yankees, Saratoga Trunk,* and *Mr. Deeds Goes to Town.* In many roles, he portrayed a "strong, silent type," and it was a running joke that his script lines often consisted merely of saying "Yup." Although his testimony before the committee contained terms somewhat more profound than "yup," it lacked much specific information about alleged subversion in Hollywood. Committee investigator H. A. Smith asked Cooper:

> SMITH: What do you believe the principal medium is that they use [in] Hollywood or the industry to inject propaganda?
> COOPER: I believe it is done through word of mouth and through the medium of pamphleting—and writers, I suppose.
> SMITH: By "word of mouth," what do you mean, Mr. Cooper?
> COOPER: Well, I mean sort of social gatherings.
> SMITH: Can you tell us some of the statements that you may have heard at these gatherings that you believe are communistic?
> COOPER: Well, I have heard quite a few, I think, from time to time over the years. Well, I have heard tossed around such statements as, "Don't you think

the Constitution of the United States is about a hundred and fifty years out of date?" And, oh, I don't know, I heard people mention that, well, "Perhaps this would be a more efficient government without a Congress"—which statements I think are very un-American.

After taking the testimony of such "friendly" witnesses as Cooper, Reagan, Taylor, Menjou, and Mrs. Rogers, the committee moved on to hear from a group of Hollywood figures considered "unfriendly" to the investigation. Most of the attention centered on ten witnesses originally known as "the Unfriendly Ten" and eventually as "the Hollywood Ten." They were movie producer Adrian Scott, director Edward Dmytryk, and screen writers John Howard Lawson, Dalton Trumbo, Ring Lardner, Jr., Albert Maltz, Alvah Bessie, Herbert Biberman, Lester Cole, and Samuel Ornitz. Most of them would eventually concede publicly—but not before the committee—that they had been communists at one time or another. They contended that the First Amendment's guarantees of freedom of speech and freedom of association barred the committee from asking them whether they belonged to the Communist Party or any other organization. They retained as their chief lawyer Robert Kenny, a former California attorney general, who advised them to refuse to answer such questions on First Amendment grounds. This strategy touched off numerous clashes between the witnesses and the committee.

The first "unfriendly" witness called by the committee was John Howard Lawson, who testified on October 27, 1947. Lawson, described by the committee as one of Hollywood's leading communists, had written the screenplays for such films as *Blockade, Algiers, Action in the North*

[68]

Atlantic, and *Counter-Attack.* At the outset of his testimony, Lawson clashed with Chairman J. Parnell Thomas by insisting on being allowed to read a prepared statement before answering any questions. Thomas glanced at the statement, which was sharply critical of the committee, and denied permission for Lawson to read it into the record.

The statement was, however, released to the press by Lawson. It said in part:

> For a week, this committee has conducted an illegal and indecent trial of American citizens, whom the committee has selected to be publicly pilloried and smeared. I am not here to defend myself or to answer the agglomeration of falsehoods that has been heaped upon me. I believe lawyers describe this material, rather mildly, as "hearsay evidence." To the American public, it has a shorter name: dirt. . . .
>
> I am plastered with mud because I happen to be an American who expresses opinions that the House Un-American Activities Committee does not like. But my opinions are not an issue in this case. The issue is my right to have opinions. . . .

When Thomas refused to allow reading of the statement into the record, Lawson protested that "friendly" witnesses had been permitted to read lengthy statements. "The rights of American citizens are important in this room here and I intend to stand up for those rights, Congressman Thomas," Lawson said. But Thomas declined to change his ruling, and directed Counsel Stripling to begin questioning Lawson.

STRIPLING: What is your occupation, Mr. Lawson?
LAWSON: I am a writer.

[69]

STRIPLING: How long have you been a writer?

LAWSON: All my life—at least thirty-five years—my adult life.

STRIPLING: Are you a member of the Screen Writers Guild?

LAWSON: The raising of any question here in regard to memberships, political beliefs or affiliation is absolutely beyond the powers of this committee. . . .

(Chairman Thomas pounded his gavel for order.)

LAWSON: It is a matter of public record that I am a member of the Screen Writers Guild.

STRIPLING: Now, Mr. Chairman, I am going to request that you instruct the witness to be responsive to the questions. . . .

LAWSON: I am not on trial here, Mr. Chairman. This committee is on trial here before the American people. Let us get that straight.

THOMAS: We don't want you to be on trial.

STRIPLING: Mr. Lawson, how long have you been a member of the Screen Writers Guild?

LAWSON: Since it was founded in its present form, in 1933.

STRIPLING: Have you ever held office in the guild?

LAWSON: The question of whether I have held office is also a question which is beyond the purview of this committee. It is an invasion of the right of association under the Bill of Rights of this country. . . .

THOMAS: The Chair will determine what is in the purview of this committee.

LAWSON: My rights as an American citizen are no less than the responsibilities of this committee of Congress. . . .

THOMAS: Mr. Lawson, you will have to stop or you

[70]

will leave the witness stand. And you will leave the witness stand because you are in contempt. . . .

LAWSON: I am glad you have made it perfectly clear that you are going to threaten and intimidate the witness, Mr. Chairman. I am an American and I am not at all easy to intimidate, and don't think I am.

(Thomas again pounded his gavel.) . . .

STRIPLING: Would you list some of the pictures which you have written the script for?

LAWSON: . . . You don't have to bring me here three thousand miles to find out what pictures I have written. The pictures that I have written are very well known. . . .

(Stripling led Lawson through a list of many of the films for which he had written the screenplays. Then Stripling asked the key question:)

STRIPLING: Mr. Lawson, are you now or have you ever been a member of the Communist Party of the United States?

LAWSON: The question here relates not only to the question of my membership in any political organization, but this committee is attempting to establish the right—

(Thomas banged his gavel still again.) . . .

THOMAS: Mr. Lawson, just quiet down again. Mr. Lawson, the most pertinent question that we can ask is whether or not you have ever been a member of the Communist Party. Now, do you care to answer that question?

LAWSON: You are using the old technique, which was used in Hitler Germany, in order to create a scare here in order to create an entirely false atmosphere in which this hearing is conducted in order that you

[71]

can then smear the motion-picture industry, and you can proceed to the press, to any form of communication in this country. . . .

THOMAS: We are going to get the answer to that question if we have to stay here for a week. Are you a member of the Communist Party or have you ever been a member of the Communist Party? . . ,

LAWSON: I am framing my answer in the only way in which any American citizen can frame his answer to a question which absolutely invades his rights.

THOMAS: Then you refuse to answer that question; is that correct? . . . Officers, take this man away from the stand—

A mixture of applause and boos poured from the spectators' gallery as officers escorted Lawson away from the witness chair. When order was restored, committee investigator Louis J. Russell was sworn as a witness, and read into the record various items purporting to show that Lawson was a communist. He said, for example, that the committee had obtained a copy of a Communist Party registration card issued in Lawson's name. He also cited articles written by Lawson for the *Daily Worker* and testimony by other witnesses who claimed they had attended Communist Party meetings with Lawson.

The following day, Dalton Trumbo was called as a witness. Trumbo, one of the highest-paid writers in Hollywood, had a contract with Metro-Goldwyn-Mayer studios permitting him to choose between a $3,000-a-week salary for as long as it took him to write a picture or a flat $75,000 fee for each script. He had already written such films as *Kitty Foyle, A Guy Named Joe, Thirty Seconds over Tokyo*, and *Our Vines Have Tender Grapes*, and would later write others such as *Exodus, Spartacus,* and *The Brave One.*

Like Lawson, Trumbo quickly became embroiled in a controversy with Chairman Thomas when he sought permission to read a prepared statement into the record, which was an indictment of the committee's abuse of constitutional rights.

After reading Trumbo's statement, Chairman Thomas told him: "Mr. Trumbo, we have looked over this statement very carefully. . . . We have concluded, and unanimously so, that this statement is not pertinent to the inquiry. Therefore, the Chair will rule that the statement will not be read." Trumbo replied:

TRUMBO: The Chair has considered a statement from Gerald L. K. Smith [a racist hatemonger who had previously testified before the committee] to be pertinent to its inquiries.

THOMAS: That statement is out of order.

TRUMBO: And where is mine different from that, sir?

THOMAS: As a witness, if you conduct yourself like the first witness yesterday [Lawson], you won't be given the privilege of being a witness before a committee of Congress, before this committee of Congress. Go ahead, Mr. Stripling.

Throughout the questioning, Thomas, Stripling, and Trumbo remained embattled, amidst much gavel pounding. Trumbo continued to try to introduce evidence into the record—statements by responsible persons concerning the character of his work, as well as his twenty scripts themselves—all to no avail. He also continued to assert his

[73]

right to membership in unions, the right not to answer questions as to his affiliations, and the right to see the committee's alleged evidence that he was a card-carrying member of the Communist Party. As Trumbo would not yield, like Lawson he was "excused" from the witness stand with Thomas remarking of his behavior: "This is typical communist tactics."

Trumbo was followed as a witness on October 29, 1947, by Edward Dmytryk, who had directed such films as *Behind the Rising Sun, Tender Comrade, Till the End of Time, Back to Bataan, Cornered, Crossfire,* and *Murder, My Sweet.* Before the questioning of Dmytryk began, Chairman Thomas opened the day's proceedings with a statement defending the committee's activities in Hollywood that apparently was prompted by criticism voiced against the investigation conducted to that point. The defense read in part:

Responding to the demand of the people, the present Committee on Un-American Activities made a preliminary investigation which produced ample evidence that a full-scale investigation was in order of the extent of communist infiltration in Hollywood. . . . The committee's authority to conduct such an investigation . . . is crystal-clear. We have not violated and we are not violating the rights of any American citizen, not even the rights of communists whose first allegiance is to a foreign government. The committee is well aware that powerful influences have sought in every manner to divert this committee from its main course of inquiry. I am proud to say that this committee has not been swayed. . . . The people are going to get the facts. . . .

Stripling then began the questioning, which again followed the pattern of that used with Lawson and Trumbo. The primary issue was whether he was or had ever been a member of the Communist Party. The testimony concluded as follows:

DMYTRYK: I have been advised that there is a question of constitutional rights involved. The Constitution does not ask that such a question be answered in the way that Mr. Stripling wants it answered. I think that what organizations I belong to, what I think and what I say cannot be questioned by this committee.

STRIPLING: Then you refuse to answer the question?

DMYTRYK: I do not refuse to answer it. I answered it in my own way.

STRIPLING: You haven't answered whether or not you are a member of the Communist Party.

DMYTRYK: I answered by saying I do not think you have the right to ask—

STRIPLING: Mr. Chairman, it is apparent that the witness is pursuing the same line as the other witnesses.

THOMAS: The witness is excused.

Dmytryk left the witness chair without indulging in further byplay with the congressmen or committee staff members. Called as a witness the next day was Ring Lardner, Jr., the son of the distinguished newspaperman and author. The younger Lardner was a $2,000-a-week screen writer who had won an Academy Award for his script for *Woman of the Year* and would later write such films as *The Cincinnati Kid* and *M*A*S*H*. When Lardner tried to read an opening statement to the committee,

Chairman Thomas ruled he could not read it until after answering the committee's questions. Stripling then asked: "Mr. Lardner, are you a member of the Screen Writers Guild?"

> LARDNER: Mr. Stripling, I want to be cooperative about this but there are certain limits to my cooperation. I don't want to help you divide or smash this particular guild, or to infiltrate the motion-picture business in any way for the purpose which seems to me to be to try to control that business, to control what the American people can see and hear in their motion-picture theaters. . . .

Thus began an altercation among Lardner, Thomas, and Stripling. At one point, Lardner said: "It seems to me you are trying to discredit the Screen Writers Guild through me, and the motion-picture industry through the Screen Writers Guild, and our whole practice of freedom of expression." Stripling then moved on to the central question of Lardner's membership in the Communist Party, with similar results. Thomas eventually said: "It is a very simple question. Anybody would be proud to answer it— any real American would be proud to answer [that] question. . . ." Lardner retorted: "It depends on the circumstances. I could answer it, but if I did I would hate myself in the morning."

Lardner was forcibly removed from the witness chair by a policeman, and committee investigator Louis Russell took the stand and testified about Lardner's alleged communist activities. He said he had found evidence that a Communist Party registration card for 1944 had been made out in Lardner's name and that it indicated he had been a subscriber to the *Daily Worker*.

The testimony of the remaining six members of the Hollywood Ten—Alvah Bessie, Herbert Biberman, Lester Cole, Albert Maltz, Samuel Ornitz, and Adrian Scott—followed the pattern established by Lawson, Trumbo, Dmytryk, and Lardner. All refused to testify whether they were or had ever been members of the Communist Party. For their refusal, all ten were cited for contempt of Congress by the Un-American Activities Committee. The full House overwhelmingly voted to uphold the citations.

All ten were convicted in trials in U.S. District Court. Eight of them were given the maximum sentence, a year in jail and a $1,000 fine. The other two, Biberman and Dmytryk, received six-month jail terms and $1,000 fines. The convictions were appealed on the grounds that the committee did not have the power to inquire into the defendants' political beliefs and that the defendants' First Amendment right to free speech included the right to remain silent.

It was not until June 13, 1949, that the U.S. Court of Appeals for the District of Columbia denied the appeals. The court ruled:

> We expressly hold herein that the House Committee on Un-American Activities, or a properly appointed subcommittee thereof, has the power to inquire whether a witness subpoenaed by it is or is not a member of the Communist Party or a believer in communism and that this power carries with it necessarily the power to effect criminal punishment for failure or refusal to answer that question. . . . To hold otherwise would indeed be holding that the power to inquire is a "powerless power." . . . [Previous court decisions] leave it no longer subject to the

[77]

slightest doubt that the committee was and is con-
stitutionally created, that it functions under valid
statute and resolution which have repeatedly and
without exception been upheld as constitutional, that
the "question under inquiry" by the committee was
proper. . . .

The decision was appealed to the U.S. Supreme Court,
but the high court declined to review the case. As a result,
the members of the Hollywood Ten surrendered in June
1950 and began serving their jail sentences.

Meanwhile, shortly after the Hollywood Ten had originally testified, fifty of the nation's most important movie
producers had met secretly at the Waldorf-Astoria hotel
in New York to decide how to cope with the bad image
Hollywood was receiving from the allegations of communism in the motion-picture industry. The meeting resulted
in an announcement that the producers had unanimously
agreed to fire the members of the Hollywood Ten, claiming their "actions have been a disservice to their employers
and have impaired their usefulness to the industry." The
producers said none of the fired men would be rehired
until he had cleared himself of contempt of Congress,
been found not guilty, or declared under oath that he was
not a communist. The decision, however, applied to far
more movie-industry employees than merely the members
of the Hollywood Ten. The producers shortly informed the
industry that all unrepenting communists—that is, those
who had not admitted and renounced their communist
affiliations—would henceforth be considered ineligible for
employment.

Thus began the notorious Hollywood blacklist.

SOURCES AND SUPPLEMENTARY READING

Published transcripts of the House Un-American Activities Committee and Eric Bentley's *Thirty Years of Treason* were primary source materials for this chapter.

Dalton Trumbo's appearance before the committee is described, with its background and aftermath, in *Additional Dialogue*. Ring Lardner, Jr., has described his experiences concerning the witch-hunt era in interviews with newspapers and magazines and in a magazine article, "My Life on the Blacklist," published by the *Saturday Evening Post*, in the October 14, 1961, issue.

Frank Donner's *The Un-Americans* contains further background on the Hollywood investigations.

7

★ ★ ★

Dark Days
of the Blacklist

Once the Hollywood blacklist was established, it gradually expanded until it encompassed hundreds of persons. They included actors, actresses, writers, directors, technicians, and even secretaries and clerks thrown out of work by the movie studios. Not only admitted or accused communists but also persons merely suspected of subversive activities were victimized by the blacklist.

It is a serious matter at any time for a person to be fired from his job. But when he is also denied the opportunity to find another job in his chosen field, his problems are multiplied many times. Severe hardships were imposed on many former movie-industry employees and their families. Some of those who had been paid extremely high salaries in the entertainment industry found themselves forced to scrape out meager livings in new occupations such as bartending, waiting on tables, driving school buses, selling clothing, and performing minor repair chores. Several, including character actor Philip Loeb, committed suicide.

A few of the blacklisted screen writers managed to find periodic work writing films under assumed names for independent producers who were not connected with the major movie studios. But they were paid only a fraction of their former earnings and were forced to resort to all manner of subterfuge to keep these writing projects secret. Blacklisted actors and actresses, of course, had no way to disguise their identities in film roles—so no comparable secret work was open to them. Their best hope for employment in their chosen profession involved competing for the relatively small number of roles available in the Broadway theater, which did not employ a blacklist.

Gradually, some persons already on the blacklist or threatened with being placed on it began seeking means of clearing themselves for further employment in the movie studios. Chiefly, they did so by agreeing to cooperate with the committee. In typical cases, they were expected to "confess" that they had belonged to subversive organizations in the past, but had now seen the error of their ways and broken with such groups. However, merely testifying about their own activities was usually not sufficient to satisfy the committee. They were also expected to identify other persons who had participated in the activities with them. Some witnesses felt they would be becoming "informers" if they testified about their former associates, and were most reluctant to do so. But they knew their careers might be destroyed if they failed to give the committee complete cooperation. The situation forced many a witness to struggle with his conscience.

Among the first Hollywood figures to be confronted with the dilemma was actor Larry Parks, who was called

[81]

before the committee in March 1951. After a relatively undistinguished acting career, Parks had scored a major success in the role of entertainer Al Jolson in the film *The Jolson Story*. He was at the height of his popularity when he was threatened with blacklisting as a result of allegedly subversive affiliations, and he appeared before the committee.

By that time, J. Parnell Thomas was no longer chairman of the committee or even a congressman. He had resigned his House seat in 1950 after being convicted of padding his congressional payroll with the names of fictitious employees and pocketing the money paid by the government for their ostensible salaries. Thomas was given a federal prison term, and ironically served his time at the U.S. penitentiary in Danbury, Connecticut, as a fellow convict of two members of the Hollywood Ten, Ring Lardner, Jr., and Lester Cole. Meanwhile, the Democrats had regained control of Congress, and Democratic Representative John Wood of Georgia, who had been Thomas's predecessor as head of the committee, returned to the chairmanship. Robert Stripling had resigned his job as the committee's chief counsel and had been replaced by an attorney named Frank S. Tavenner, Jr.

It was Tavenner who led the questioning when Larry Parks appeared before the committee. Parks admitted early in the questioning that he was a former communist, and Tavenner then asked why he had become a member of the party.

> PARKS: Being a member of the Communist Party fulfilled certain needs of a young man that was liberal in thought, idealistic, who was for the underprivileged, the underdog. . . . I think that being a com-

munist in 1951 in this particular situation [the United States was then fighting communist forces in the Korean War] is an entirely different kettle of fish, when this [communism] is a great power that is trying to take over the world. This is the difference. . . ."

The testimony continued as Tavenner asked details of how, when, and where Parks had joined the party, the extent of his activity as a member, and who else was involved in his particular cell group. Parks began sparring intermittently with Tavenner and committee members over whether he should be compelled to identify persons who had belonged to the Communist Party with him. It was an issue that persisted throughout his testimony.

At one point, Parks pleaded: "Don't present me with the choice of either being in contempt of this committee and going to jail or forcing me to really crawl through the mud to become an informer." Ultimately, the committee decided to hear the remainder of Parks's testimony in executive session (closed to the public and the press). The committee's theory was that Parks might be more willing to provide names in a closed session. Testimony so taken is not made public unless a congressional committee decides there is some expedient reason for releasing it. In Parks's case, the committee waited two years before releasing the executive-session testimony—but when he gave it he had no idea when, if at all, it would be made public. The committee strategy succeeded in persuading him to provide the desired names.

Tavenner asked him during the executive session: "Who were the members of the Communist Party cell to which you were assigned during the period from 1941 until 1945?"

Parks replied: "Well, Morris Carnovsky, Joe Bromberg, Sam Rossen, Anne Revere, Lee Cobb, Gale Sondergaard, Dorothy Tree. Those are the principal names that I recall."

But the committee was not satisfied merely to have the names of Parks's cell members. Tavenner pressed further about who had attended meetings with him, and who else might possibly be or have been involved in alleged communist activities. He then threw out name after name in the questioning; among others, Tavenner's list included Howard Da Silva, Roman Bohnen (who was then dead), James Cagney, Sam Jaffe, John Garfield, Sterling Hayden, Andy Devine, Madeleine Carroll, Gregory Peck, Humphrey Bogart, and Edward G. Robinson.

Parks's testimony ended. His reluctant decision to name some names resulted in several members of the committee publicly praising him. Republican Congressman Harold H. Velde of Illinois, for example, took the House floor and described Parks as both "a great actor" and "a loyal and true American." Such praise was generally regarded as a clue to movie studios that it was "safe" to employ Parks— that they would not be criticized by the committee or its supporters for failure to blacklist him.

An interesting question is why the committee chose to drop into the questioning the names of some persons about whom Parks could provide no information. A number of those persons, including such big-name stars as Humphrey Bogart and Gregory Peck, apparently had never done anything more subversive than raise objections to the committee's methods or support worthy causes that were also coincidentally backed by communists. It would appear that these names were introduced merely for the publicity value they could bring the committee when Parks's executive-session testimony was eventually made public.

[84]

One star about whom Parks said he could give no information, Edward G. Robinson, later described the way ill-founded charges against him had damaged his career during the blacklisting period. In an interview with the *New York Times* in 1971, Robinson said:

> Suddenly, around 1950–1951, I found I couldn't get work. I was handed lousy B-picture assignments. Those goons, those vigilantes and so-called "good Americans," confused some of us with really sinister, genuine communists in our midst. It was true that I had supported various pro-Russian organizations during World War II. But who hadn't? We were supposed to be Russia's ally, weren't we?
>
> I was never subpoenaed by the House Committee. . . . I decided to do something about it and go before the committee voluntarily to clear my name. They said, "We have nothing on you." But I was sure they thought they had. I demanded to be put under oath. They refused. I insisted. Finally, they agreed. I told them I was clean. They accepted that. But the press still kept bandying my name around. I went back and once again they commended my action. But the implications went on and on. . . .
>
> The shadow hung over me for six years. Finally, [producer] Cecil B. DeMille decided he wanted me for a part in *The Ten Commandments*. He said, "I've had you investigated, and you're as clean as a hound's tooth." He reinstated me, but it was only a character role. That whole period was a bad dream.

Following Larry Parks's appearance before the committee, various other Hollywood figures took the witness chair and admitted past Communist Party membership or participation in other activities regarded by the committee as subversive. Actor Sterling Hayden testified that he had been a party member for five or six months during 1946, and provided the committee with the names of those he said had taken part in party activities with him. Although he seemed to show no reluctance during his testimony, Hayden afterward wrote in his autobiography, *Wanderer*, that he later came to think of himself as a "stoolie." In a passage addressed to his psychoanalyst, he wrote: "I don't think you have the foggiest notion of the contempt I have had for myself since the day I did that thing."

The noted film and stage director Elia Kazan admitted to the committee that he had been a Communist Party member for about eighteen months during the 1930s. In his initial appearance before the committee, Kazan declined to talk about other persons who had belonged to the party with him. But three months later, he changed his mind and made a voluntary second appearance before the committee in which he identified those he said had been his fellow party members. In a statement to the committee, Kazan said: "I have come to the conclusion that I did wrong to withhold these names before, because secrecy serves the communists and is exactly what they want."

The day after his second appearance before the committee, Kazan took the unusual step of buying advertising space in the *New York Times* to explain at length his past party membership, his break with the party, and his decision to identify his former communist colleagues. Some of Kazan's critics claimed the advertisement and his testimony before the committee were motivated by a desire to avoid the blacklist, rather than a genuine zeal to expose

[86]

the ills of communism. Kazan was far from alone in being accused of such motives after providing cooperative testimony to the committee. Among the others was director Edward Dmytryk.

Like his fellow members of the Hollywood Ten, Dmytryk had been blacklisted shortly after his initial appearance before the committee. Unlike some of the others, who were able to find secret film work under assumed names, Dmytryk endured a long period of unemployment. Finally, on April 25, 1951, he made a voluntary return appearance before the committee—where he testified that he had been a Communist Party member from "sometime around the spring or early summer 1944 until about the fall of 1945." He also named a handful of Hollywood personalities he said had been his fellow party members, all of whom had previously been identified as alleged communists before the committee.

Following his testimony, Dmytryk was removed from the blacklist and permitted to resume his motion-picture career. Among those who accused Dmytryk of cooperating with the committee strictly in the interest of winning a release from the blacklist was another member of the Hollywood Ten, Albert Maltz. In a letter to the *Saturday Evening Post*, which had published an article about Dmytryk's supposed turn away from communism, Maltz wrote: "The truth about Dmytryk is simple and ugly. He believed in certain principles, no doubt very sincerely, until the consequences of those beliefs became painful. He has not now made a peace with his conscience; he has made it with his pocketbook and his career."

Not only Hollywood personalities who were or had been actual Communist Party members, but also some who had lent their prestigious names to organizations accused of supporting causes fostered by the communists, were called before the investigating committee. Many of the non-communists testified they had backed such organizations without being fully aware of the groups' goals. Typical of these witnesses was actor José Ferrer. In 1950, when Ferrer was nominated for an Academy Award for his film role as Cyrano de Bergerac, Hollywood conservatives tried to deny him the award on the ground that he was active in allegedly subversive organizations. Ferrer bought newspaper advertisements, denying he was a communist, and ultimately won the Oscar. On May 22, 1951, Ferrer was called to testify, and after completing his testimony, he was able to continue his career without fear of being blacklisted.

Other witnesses during this period were not so cooperative. One who declined to answer questions from the committee was the noted playwright and screen writer Lillian Hellman. A previous witness, film writer Martin Berkeley, had testified that Miss Hellman had been among those attending a 1937 meeting at which a Hollywood section of the Communist Party had been organized. When subpoenaed by the Un-American Activities Committee in 1952, Miss Hellman wrote a letter to Chairman Wood saying she would be willing to answer questions about her own activities but not about other persons. She said, however, that her attorney had warned her she could be cited for contempt of Congress if she answered some questions and not others. Therefore, if the committee insisted on pressing her to testify about other persons, she would plead the Fifth Amendment in response to questions about both herself and the others. The Fifth Amendment to the Constitution provides that a witness cannot be compelled to testify against himself. A year before Miss Hellman was subpoenaed, the Supreme Court had ruled that a person who admitted having been a Communist Party member automatically waived use of the Fifth Amendment and could be cited for contempt if he withheld additional facts —such as the names of other party members.

Chairman Wood wrote to Miss Hellman that "the committee cannot permit witnesses to set forth the terms under which they will testify." When Miss Hellman was called before the committee, she pleaded the Fifth Amendment in response to questions both about herself and about other individuals.

Her refusal to answer the questions made her subject to blacklisting by the movie industry. Meanwhile, hundreds of other motion-picture employees remained on the blacklist. Moreover, the practice of blacklisting had spread to the radio and television industries.

There was an especially sinister quality about the radio-TV blacklist. Private, self-appointed groups set themselves up as clearance agencies capable of determining—for the payment of fees—who should be eligible to appear on television and radio broadcasts. These agencies sold their services to the networks, producers, and advertising agencies. They maintained voluminous files, often based on faulty information or the worst kind of hearsay, regarding the supposedly subversive backgrounds of persons in the entertainment business. When a person was being considered for a broadcast role, his prospective employer would submit his name to one of the clearance agencies. A performer rejected for a role was never told that he was blacklisted; instead he was given some other excuse.

The clearance agencies were closely allied with some of the major television and radio advertisers. Thus, a network or a producer trying to employ a blacklisted performer

[89]

faced the prospect of having an advertiser withdraw the financial sponsorship that kept a program on the air.

Many of those blacklisted from broadcasting jobs—including not only performers but also writers and behind-the-scenes workers—felt helpless to combat the situation. They did not know how to prove that a blacklist existed, much less that it was responsible for denying them employment. As a result, they sought work in other fields. But occasionally someone decided to fight the blacklist. One notable case involved a radio personality named John Henry Faulk.

In 1956, Faulk was the star of a daily one-hour program on WCBS in New York—the leading station of the Columbia Broadcasting System. As Faulk would later describe the show: "I spun a few yarns, reminisced about my childhood in Texas and commented on the news of the day and the foibles of the world." On February 10, 1956, a clearance agency called AWARE, INC., published a bulletin accusing Faulk of performing for or being affiliated with several allegedly subversive organizations. A short time later, Faulk was fired from his job and found himself unable to obtain other radio work. It seemed clear that he had been blacklisted.

Faulk filed a lawsuit against AWARE and its top officials, accusing them of falsely representing his background in their bulletin and causing him to be blacklisted. Evidence produced at the trial of the lawsuit disclosed that AWARE officials had used slipshod methods in compiling information about Faulk and other performers, and had applied pressure to radio advertisers to keep Faulk off the air. A jury awarded Faulk a $3,500,000 judgment against the defendants, but appellate courts later found that amount excessive and ordered the defendants to pay him $550,000.

Even so, a judgment of more than a half-million dollars represented a major victory over the blacklisters.

Meanwhile, other cracks appeared in the blacklisting system. In 1956, *The Brave One* was chosen for the Academy Award as the best-written screenplay of the year. Listed as the writer, and thus the winner of the Oscar, was someone called Robert Rich. But when Rich's name was announced at the award ceremonies, nobody stepped forward to claim the prize. And nobody seemed to know who Robert Rich was. A great mystery developed over his identity. Eventually, it was disclosed that Robert Rich was one of many assumed names used by Dalton Trumbo, one of the Hollywood Ten, in secretly selling movie scripts to independent producers. The Academy of Motion Picture Arts and Sciences, which administers the Academy Awards, ruled that no award could be presented to anyone who had refused to testify before a congressional committee. The incident caused the motion-picture industry great embarrassment, pointing up the ridiculous and yet harmful nature of the blacklist. Three years later, the Academy of Motion Picture Arts and Sciences rescinded the 1956 rule.

In 1958, Trumbo was assigned to write the screenplay— under his own name—for the film *Spartacus*. The picture was produced by Byna Productions, headed by actor Kirk Douglas, for release by a major studio, Universal Pictures. The decision to give Trumbo full screen credit for the script was not immediately made public. But a short time later, one of Hollywood's best-known producers, Otto Preminger, announced that Trumbo would write the screenplay for *Exodus*, and Trumbo's authorship of *Spartacus* was soon revealed. Such disclosures marked significant steps in bringing the blacklist to an end. It gradually withered away, as increasing numbers of formerly black-listed persons were able to obtain jobs in films, radio, and television.

But that in no way made up for the fact that, for more than a decade, incalculable harm had been done to hundreds of careers by the blacklist. There was no way of bringing back the years that, for all intents and purposes, had been lost to many of the blacklisted.

SOURCES AND SUPPLEMENTARY READING

As in chapter 6, transcripts of House Un-American Activities Committee hearings and Eric Bentley's *Thirty Years of Treason* were primary sources.

Edward G. Robinson's interview with the *New York Times* in 1971, while it concerned the broad range of his life, provided fresh insight into the manner in which the witch-hunt era scarred the careers of renowned entertainers.

Walter Goodman's *The Committee* and Frank J. Donner's *The Un-Americans* helped place the Hollywood investigations in historical perspective.

Fear on Trial by John Henry Faulk (Simon and Schuster, 1964) is a moving, well-documented account of how the blacklisters came close to ruining one performer's career. I commend it highly, although some of the testimony may seem a bit heavy and the legal terminology complex; however, it provides an intriguing look at the off-screen activities of some performers still popular today. In particular, it discusses with clarity and fairness the internal union battles that saw some performers participate in what can only be described as a plot to keep others with differing political views from appearing on television and radio. Further, it describes the courage and integrity of those who dared great pressure to defend Faulk and fight the blacklist—among them David Susskind, Garry Moore, Tony Randall, and such newscasters as Charles Collingwood and the late Edward R. Murrow.

8

★ ★ ★

The Chambers–Hiss Case

Although HUAC spent a good deal of time investigating alleged subversion in the entertainment world during the late 1940s and early 1950s, its activities were by no means confined to that subject. During that period, the committee also conducted investigations covering a wide range of other fields.

To examine some of those investigations, it is necessary to flash back to 1948 after the hearings of the Hollywood Ten. Congressman J. Parnell Thomas, whose padding of his government payroll had not yet been discovered, was still chairman of the committee; Robert Stripling was still chief counsel. Thomas appointed California Congressman Richard Nixon to head a subcommittee investigating the need to pass legislation "to curb or control the Communist Party of the United States." It was one of the committee's few efforts to make serious studies of proposed legislation. Two bills were under consideration—one that proposed to outlaw the Communist Party and the other requiring the party and its front groups to register with the government. The registration bill was generally given greater odds of passage on the theory that it would expose the identities of alleged subversives and prevent them from carrying on underground activities.

Batteries of witnesses testified for and against the two bills. Speaking for the Truman administration, Attorney General Tom Clark showed enthusiasm for neither bill but said that, if he had to choose between them, he would prefer the registration measure. The most colorful witness was Arthur Garfield Hays, general counsel of the American Civil Liberties Union, who vigorously opposed both bills.

Hays, a distinguished lawyer, poked fun at the proposed legislation by submitting for the subcommittee's consideration a mock bill of his own. The measure, "a bill to provide means to eliminate the communist nuisance," included some of the following provisions:

> Whereas this was a happy land with no troubles until hordes of communists overran us, causing high prices, strikes, conspiracies and treason; and . . .
>
> Whereas experience during the late war proved conclusively that the FBI, the police, the military and all of our courts and laws are incapable of doing their jobs of apprehending traitors; . . . Therefore be it
>
> Enacted by the Senate and House of Representatives of the United States in Congress assembled: . . .
>
> 1. That we appropriate $10 billion to set up a commission to invent a mental reading machine which when applied will say "communist" when the individual is not a loyal citizen.
>
> 2. Until such machine is fully developed, all com-

munists must wear boots, red shirts, fur caps (both male and female) and grow beards (both male and female).

Needless to say, subcommittee members saw no humor in Hays's mock proposal. For his part, after reading the tongue-in-cheek bill, Hays dealt in a more serious vein with the actual legislation under consideration:

> In my judgment no [anticommunist] laws should be passed. It is about time our legislators realized that the American people are to be trusted and need no laws to save them from bad propaganda or bad thinking. After one hundred fifty years of history, our people have shown that they are entitled to be trusted. . . . We should let people alone to think, talk and develop propaganda as they choose. We should encourage those of radical thought to come out into the open and to act along political lines. If their views are obnoxious, it is the American belief that they will not get very far.

Republican Congressman John McDowell of Pennsylvania called Hays's views "startling," and Democratic Congressman F. Edward Hébert of Louisiana told Hays: "When a disease is spreading either on the body politic or the human body, it behooves us as intelligent human beings to do something to retard it."

Despite arguments, the subcommittee and the full Un-American Activities Committee approved a bill to "protect the United States against un-American and subversive activities." The measure would have required the Communist Party and its front organizations to register with the government. The attorney general would have been placed in charge of designating which groups would be required to register. When the bill reached the House floor, a small band of opponents argued that the measure would be unconstitutional. But Congressman Nixon, who was serving as the floor manager for supporters of the legislation, knew he had the votes to push the bill through the House. When the vote was taken, the measure was approved by a margin of 319 to 58. In the Senate, however, there was no great enthusiasm for the bill. The congressional session ended without the Senate's taking action on the measure.

Meanwhile, HUAC returned to the subject of alleged subversion within the federal government—one of the entries in its eight-point program established in 1947. It chose as its next target Dr. Edward Condon, director of the National Bureau of Standards, a branch of the Commerce Department whose official duties are defined as "assuring maximum application of the physical and engineering sciences to the advancement of technology in industry and commerce." Condon, one of the nation's leading physicists, had played an important role in the development of the atomic bomb.

Committee Chairman Thomas, without even conducting any hearings, issued what he called a preliminary report on Condon—describing him as "one of the weakest links in our atomic security." The report made a variety of vague charges against Condon. It accused him of associating with "members of the Communist Party"—but did not name any of them. It also gave the impression that there was something subversive about Condon's meeting with communist officials of East European countries, when actually his official duties required such meetings. Moreover, the report charged incorrectly that a scientific organization to which Condon belonged had been designated as subversive by the attorney general.

Nonetheless, the report resulted in widespread unfavorable publicity for Condon. Thomas apparently had been motivated to attack Condon at least in part because Condon had been one of a group of influential scientists who had been instrumental in seeing to it that control of the Atomic Energy Commission (AEC) was placed in civilian hands. Thomas and other members of his committee wanted the military to control the AEC.

The Condon affair touched off a test of strength between HUAC and the Truman administration. Thomas and many other Republicans were anxious to use the subversives-in-government issue against President Truman as he prepared to run for a full four-year term in the White House. Truman, never a man to shrink from a fight, staunchly defended Condon. Despite the allegations made against him, the Commerce Department's loyalty-review board issued Condon a full security clearance.

Nevertheless, the AEC, after reviewing all the background information compiled on Condon by the FBI and other agencies, decided to continue his security clearance, saying it was "in the best interests of the atomic energy program." Sporadic charges were made against Condon during the next several years by members of the investigating committee. When he resigned as director of the National Bureau of Standards in 1951, committee members claimed they had forced him out of office. It was not until a year later, however, that Condon was called to testify before the committee.

He was questioned about his friendships with several left-wing scientists, as well as his association with col-

[98]

leagues who earlier had pleaded the Fifth Amendment before the committee. Condon readily conceded the friendships, and also stated he had no intention of disowning former colleagues—whom he had known since youth—because of their Fifth Amendment pleas.

At most, the committee disclosed a certain amount of imprudence on Condon's part, but never came close to its earlier charge that he was a security risk. However, the committee's new report said Condon should be barred from jobs requiring security clearance because of his purported "propensity for associating with persons . . . of questionable loyalty. . . ." Condon remained a controversial figure in ensuing years, but in 1966 the U.S. Air Force named him to direct its investigations of unidentified flying objects (UFOs).

After beginning the Condon investigation in 1948—which was conducted in fits and starts over several years—the committee moved on to the subject of alleged communist espionage within the federal government.

The first major cooperative witness called by the committee was a woman named Elizabeth T. Bentley, who was dubbed "the spy queen" by some newspapers but never quite lived up to that title. Miss Bentley, who was born in 1908, was graduated from Vassar College in 1930 and received a master's degree from Columbia University in 1935, when she also joined the Communist Party. After continuing her studies in Italy and spending two years as a teacher at an exclusive girls' school in Virginia, she took a job in 1938 at the Italian Library of Information in New York.

Miss Bentley testified that she discovered the Italian Library was distributing "fascist propaganda" and that she immediately went to Communist Party headquarters in

New York to report that fact. At the headquarters, she met a man named Jacob Golos, who she later learned was a Soviet agent. A romance developed between the two—a romance that Miss Bentley said became the most important aspect of her life: "Nothing mattered anymore. I had found the man I loved."

Miss Bentley testified that she served as a courier for an espionage ring headed by Golos—traveling to Washington about every two weeks to collect material smuggled out of government files by disloyal employees.

Miss Bentley dropped many names of government officials into her testimony, leaving the implication they were somehow involved in the alleged espionage ring. But in some cases, her information about the officials was based on hearsay.

Miss Bentley offered no evidence to support her allegations, and was not asked for any. She said she continued to serve as a courier for the ring throughout most of World War II—during a large part of which the United States and the Soviet Union were allies. She said her break with communism began when Golos died in 1944.

Despite the weaknesses in her testimony, investigations sparked by Miss Bentley's allegations led to the firing of eleven State Department employees. But perhaps more important, in an attempt to substantiate some of Miss Bentley's charges, HUAC questioned a *Time* magazine editor named Whittaker Chambers, who had formerly been a communist. The questioning of Chambers touched off the most famous and controversial investigation in the committee's history, the case of Alger Hiss.

Chambers said that during the 1930s he had been a member of a secret communist group in Washington whose purpose was to place communists in influential government jobs. He identified eight former officials as members of the group. Six of the eight pleaded the Fifth Amendment when questioned by the committee about Chambers's allegations. The other two—Alger Hiss and his brother, Donald—flatly denied the charges and insisted they had never been communists.

Of those mentioned by Chambers, Alger Hiss was by far the most prominent. Although only forty-four at the time the committee began its investigation of him, Hiss had already had a distinguished career. After his graduation from Harvard Law School, where he had been an honor student, Hiss became law clerk to U.S. Supreme Court Justice Oliver Wendell Holmes. He later practiced with prestigious law firms in Boston and New York before going to Washington early in the Roosevelt administration to become an official of the Agricultural Adjustment Administration. In 1934, he became counsel to a Senate committee—the Nye committee—that made headlines with an investigation of profiteering in the munitions industry. After that, Hiss served as a special attorney in the Justice Department before taking a series of increasingly important posts in the State Department. While in the State Department, he attended several international conferences with Presidents Roosevelt and Truman and played a key role in the creation of the United Nations. He was secretary general of the international assembly in San Francisco that adopted the UN Charter, and he was given the honor of carrying the charter from San Francisco to Washington for President Truman's signature. In 1947, after leaving the government, Hiss became president of the influential Carnegie Endowment for International Peace.

Chambers's allegations were considered sensational because of the prominence of Hiss. Although Chambers did not at first charge that the purported Washington communist group had been engaged in espionage—but rather in attempts to plant members in jobs where they could influence government policy—the aura of a "spy hunt" hung over the investigation from the start. National attention quickly focused on Chambers, who had been a virtual unknown until that time.

Chambers told the committee he joined the Communist Party in 1924. He worked for a time as an editor of the left-wing magazine *New Masses*, which he called "in effect a communist organ." In 1932, Chambers said, he was called to the office of Max Bedacht, a member of the Communist Party Central Committee. He testified that Bedacht told him he was to become a member of the communist underground. "My function was to act as liaison man between the underground apparatus and the leader of the open Communist Party. The leader then was Bedacht."

Hiss was first recruited into a communist underground apparatus in Washington developed by a man named Harold Ware, Chambers said. Ware was the son of a communist leader named Ella Reeve Bloor, who was known as Mother Bloor. Chambers testified he was introduced to Hiss in late 1934 in Washington by Ware and J. Peters, a mysterious man who used many assumed names and was then head of the underground section of the U.S. Communist Party. Chambers said he became a courier between Ware's Washington group and Peters, who was headquartered in New York. But, he said, Peters also gave him an even more important assignment:

My principal function in Washington was to organize a parallel apparatus, separating some from that [Ware] group. It was very clear that some of them [members of the Ware group] were going places in the government. One was Alger Hiss. . . . These people were an elite group. It was believed they would rise to better positions in the government and would be of very much more service to the Communist Party. So it was decided by Peters, or by Peters in conference with people whom I don't know, that we would take these people out of that apparatus. That is, they would have no further intercourse with the other people there, but would still be connected with it through me and with Peters through me. The first man separated from the apparatus was Alger Hiss.

Committee members asked Chambers how he knew that Hiss was a communist. Chambers replied that J. Peters had first told him so. Congressman Richard Nixon, who was to play a major role in the Hiss investigation and use it as a stepping stone to higher political office, asked: "Do you have evidence?"

Chambers replied: "Nothing beyond the fact that he submitted himself for the two or three years that I knew him as a dedicated and disciplined communist. I collected party dues from him over two or three years. . . ."

Chambers seemed to show considerable familiarity with details of the personal lives of Hiss and Hiss's wife, Priscilla. He said that he, his wife, and their infant daughter were overnight guests several times in the Hiss home. He also testified that Hiss permitted the Chambers family to live in a Washington apartment for at least three weeks after the Hisses left there to move to another address. He spoke of the "extreme simplicity" in which members of the Hiss family lived, and of the fact that they were amateur bird-watchers.

[103]

In 1937, Chambers said, he decided that communism was "a form of totalitarianism, that its triumph means slavery to men," and that he resolved to break with the Communist Party. He claimed he lived in hiding for a year, "with a gun within easy reach," fearful of reprisals from the communists over his defection. He also claimed he tried to encourage a number of people to break with the party—including Alger Hiss.

Asked why he had made the effort to persuade Hiss, Chambers replied: "He was perhaps my closest friend, certainly the closest friend I ever had in the Communist Party. . . . I do not hate Mr. Hiss . . . but we are caught in a tragedy of history. . . ."

Chambers's initial public testimony was given on August 3, 1948. Hiss immediately issued denial of the charges and demanded an opportunity to testify before the committee. He was called to the witness chair on August 5, where he said: "I am here at my own request to deny unqualifiedly various statements about me which were made before this committee by one Whittaker Chambers."

Hiss said he had never known anyone by the name of Whittaker Chambers. "So far as I know, I have never laid eyes on him, and I should like to have the opportunity to do so." Stripling handed Hiss a recent picture of Chambers, saying Chambers had gained weight since the period when he claimed to have known Hiss. Hiss studied the picture, then said:

> I have looked at all the pictures I was able to get hold of in the newspapers. . . . He looks like a lot of people. . . . I would not want to take oath that I have never seen that man. I would like to see him.

Then I think I would be better able to tell whether I had ever seen him.

Hiss then reviewed the list of names of men described by Chambers as members of the supposed secret communist group in Washington. In addition to Hiss and his brother, Donald, a former Labor Department official, the list included four men who had served with Hiss as attorneys for the Agricultural Adjustment Administration—Lee Pressman, John Abt, Charles Kramer, and Nathan Witt; Henry Collins, a former Labor Department attorney; and Victor Perlo, a former official of the National Recovery Administration. Hiss testified as to his relationship with each of the named persons except Perlo, whom he said he did not think he knew; he asserted that the statements made by Chambers were "complete fabrications." Congressman Mundt then told Hiss he found it puzzling that both he and his brother were included in this list when "There seems to be no question about the subversive connections of the other six."

The hearing continued with Mundt, Stripling, and Nixon engaging in exchanges with Hiss. Hiss was questioned about Chambers's possible motivations; whether he had attended meetings with an alleged communist group at the apartment of Henry Collins, as Chambers had testified; what his position was on the general subject of alleged communist activity in the government; and whether he thought every effort should be made to look into such alleged subversive activity.

But the main issue before the committee was the direct conflict in the testimony of Chambers and Hiss. As Mundt put it:

The testimony is diametrically opposite and comes from two witnesses whom one would normally assume to be perfectly reliable. They both appear to be honest. They both testify under oath. Certainly, the committee and the country are badly confused about why these stories fail so completely to jibe.

Nixon proposed further hearings to try to clear up the confusion.

After the hearing was adjourned, the committee met privately to decide what to do next. Most members felt that Hiss had made a very convincing witness, that he had been telling the truth, and that the committee had been taken in by Chambers. They assumed that large segments of the press and public would accuse the committee of conducting a witch hunt or, at the very least, of unjustifiably allowing Chambers to tell his story in a public hearing before checking its accuracy. One Republican committee member said flatly: "We've been had. We're ruined." Democratic Congressman Edward Hébert of Louisiana suggested the committee try to "get off the hook" by dropping the investigation and turning its file over to the Justice Department to determine who was lying. "Let's wash our hands of the whole mess," Hébert said.

But Nixon argued against following that course. He pointed out that Hiss had never flatly denied knowing Chambers—that Hiss had always hedged his answer by saying he did not know a man "by the name of Whittaker Chambers." It was possible that Hiss had known Chambers under some other name, Nixon asserted. While the committee might not be able to prove conclusively that Hiss was a communist, he said, it might be able to find evidence showing that the two men knew each other. And if it could be shown that Hiss had lied about knowing Chambers, a strong argument could be made that he had also lied about being a communist. Committee Counsel Stripling supported Nixon's contentions.

The committee then agreed to name a subcommittee, headed by Nixon, to question Chambers further in a secret hearing to try to clear up the conflict in testimony. The hearing was conducted two days later. The only persons present were Chambers, the three subcommittee members —Nixon, Hébert, and McDowell—and five committee employees.

Nixon, seeking corroboration for Chambers's claim that he knew Hiss well, asked a long series of questions about Hiss's personal background, family, and habits. Chambers provided what appeared to be minute details. In describing this testimony, Nixon later wrote: "All of this information, I realized, he [Chambers] might have obtained by studying Hiss's life without actually knowing him. But some of the answers had a personal ring of truth about them, beyond the bare facts themselves."

As Nixon prepared to adjourn the hearing, he asked: "Would you be willing to submit to a lie-detector on this testimony?"

"Yes, if necessary," Chambers replied.

"You have that much confidence?"

"I am telling the truth."

"I have no further questions."

Nine days after Chambers's appearance at the closed hearing of the subcommittee, Hiss testified at a similar secret session. The session produced several surprising developments.

The hearing began with Nixon saying to Hiss that, given

the conflicts in the case, the committee was faced with the problem of determining which witness had given false testimony, and that it was the committee's responsibility to resolve the problem. He then asked Hiss to bear with him during the detailed questioning, even when some matters had been previously covered. Nixon said: "We want the record to be absolutely straight on your testimony and that of Mr. Chambers—on the points of variance and on the points of agreement."

Nixon pointed out that newspaper stories following Chambers's most recent testimony had reported that Chambers claimed to have used the name Carl in his alleged dealings with Hiss. The stories had been based on leaks of information from the subcommittee concerning Chambers's supposedly secret testimony. Nixon asked: "Do you recall any individual known to you between 1934 and 1938 as Carl?"

Hiss replied: "I do not recall anyone by the name of Carl who could remotely be connected with the testimony Mr. Chambers has given."

Nixon then returned to the question, raised when Hiss first testified, of whether he had visited Henry Collins's Washington apartment on St. Matthew's Court; then, whether he had seen Pressman, Witt, Abt, Kramer, and Perlo there.

The questioning then turned directly to the issue of whether Hiss knew Chambers. The committee had obtained two photographs of Chambers taken during the 1930s, and these were shown to Hiss.

NIXON: After looking at those pictures, I ask you if you can remember that person, either as Whittaker

[108]

Chambers or as Carl or as any other individual you have met?

HISS: May I recall to the committee the testimony I gave in public session when I was shown another photograph of Mr. Whittaker Chambers? I testified then that I could not swear that I had never seen the man whose picture was shown to me. Actually, the face had a certain familiarity. I think I also testified to that. It is not a very distinctive or unusual face. I would very much like to see the individual face to face. . . .

Actually, despite Hiss's statement to the contrary, this was the first time he had testified that Chambers's face had "a certain familiarity." Nixon asked if his testimony would be any different if he were told that the man in the picture had stayed overnight several times in Hiss's home. Hiss responded: "If this is a picture of anyone like that, I would find it difficult to believe that his face would not be more familiar than it is. . . . I do hope I will have an opportunity to see the individual." Nixon said a confrontation between the two men was going to be arranged.

Hiss then requested and was granted permission to make a point.

HISS: I have been angered and hurt by one thing in the course of this committee testimony. That is the attitude taken by Mr. Mundt when I testified publicly and by Mr. Nixon today. I restrained myself with some difficulty from commenting on it publicly. I would like to say it on this occasion, which is not a public hearing. . . . You and Mr. Mundt have taken the attitude that you simply have two witnesses saying contradictory things. . . . I honestly have the feeling that details of my personal life, which I give honestly, can be used to my disadvantage by Chambers if he knows them. . . . I should not be asked to give details which somehow he may hear and then may be able to use as if he knew them long before now.

NIXON: There is a very serious implication in your statement. That is, that the committee is questioning you today to get information with which we can coach Chambers so he can build a web around you.

HISS: I meant no such implication. . . .

Despite his statement that he "meant no such implication," Hiss's further testimony indicated he did indeed mean to raise the suspicion that information he provided the committee might be secretly slipped to Chambers. Nixon told him the committee had no intention of using his testimony in such a way. Committee Counsel Stripling told Hiss that Chambers had testified at great length during the executive session, and then showed Hiss another, recent photograph of Chambers.

Chairman Thomas and Nixon continued to question Hiss on the matter of identifying Chambers, and whether Chambers had spent a week with the Hiss family. Hiss repeated that he was not prepared to testify to this on the basis of a photograph. However, Hiss continued: "I am absolutely prepared to testify that nobody—that man or any other man—had any such conversation with me as Chambers has testified to."

Nixon replied: "One point is pretty clear. You have agreed that you or Mr. Chambers must have committed perjury. . . ." He then said that, although membership in the Communist Party might be concealed, there were "objective items" in connection with the relationship to Chambers which, in some cases, might be confirmed by third parties. "That, frankly, is the purpose of these questions," Nixon said.

At that point, Hiss volunteered some information that provided one of the major surprises of the day.

> HISS: I have written a name on this pad in front of me of a person I knew in 1933 and 1934 who not only spent some time in my home but sublet my apartment. I do not recognize the photographs as possibly being this man. . . . I do not want and I don't think I ought to be asked to testify now to that man's name. I have given the name to two friends of mine before I came to this hearing. Perhaps I am being over-anxious about the possibility of unauthorized disclosure of this testimony. But I don't think, in my present frame of mind, it is fair that I be asked to put on record personal facts which, if they came to the ears of someone who, for no reason I can understand, had a desire to injure me, would assist him in that endeavor.
>
> NIXON: Is this man who spent the time with you in 1933 and 1934 a man with whom you are still acquainted?
>
> HISS: He is not. He was not named Carl and not Whittaker Chambers.

For the next quarter hour, Hiss sparred with Nixon and other committee members—repeatedly returning to the point that information he gave them might he "fed" to Chambers. Finally, Congressman Hébert grew impatient with Hiss.

HEBERT: Mr. Hiss . . . I will tell you exactly what I told Mr. Chambers, so that it will be a matter of record, too. Either you or Mr. Chambers is lying . . . and whichever one of you is lying is the greatest actor that America has ever produced. Now, I have not come to the conclusion yet which one of you is lying and I am trying to find the facts. Up to a few minutes ago, you have been very open, very cooperative. Now, you have hedged. . . .

HISS: It is difficult for me to control myself. That you can sit there, Mr. Hébert, and say to me casually that you have heard that man and you have heard me and you just have no basis for judging which one is telling the truth. I don't think a judge determines the credibility of witnesses on that basis.

HÉBERT: I absolutely have an open mind and am trying to give you as fair a hearing as I could possibly give Chambers or yourself. The fact that Mr. Chambers is a self-confessed traitor . . . and a self-confessed former member of the Communist Party has no bearing at all on the alleged facts he has told—

Hiss again argued that the real issue was not whether he and Chambers had known each other, but whether they had taken part in the purported conversation, in which Chambers claimed he had tried to talk Hiss into quitting the Communist Party. After a few more minutes of relatively unimportant questioning, the committee took a brief recess. During that respite, Hiss decided to disclose the name he had written on the note pad in front of him. When the hearing resumed, Hiss did not even wait to be asked any questions. He simply blurted out: "The name of the man I brought in—and he may have no relation to this nightmare—is a man named George Crosley. I met him when I was working for the Nye committee. He was a writer. He hoped to sell articles to magazines about the munitions industry."

Hiss said Crosley began hanging around the Nye committee offices, seeking information for his articles. "I saw him as I saw dozens of other representatives of the press, people writing books and research people," he testified.

Asked whether he had ever discussed politics with Crosley, Hiss replied: "Quite frequently. May I state that it was not the custom in Washington in those days, when a member of the press called on you, to ask him whether or not he was a communist."

Over a period of five or six months, Hiss said, he saw Crosley perhaps ten or eleven times. In May 1935, the Hiss family moved from an apartment on Twenty-eighth Street in Washington to a home on P Street. But the lease on the apartment had several months to run and Hiss was obliged to pay the rent. During that period, Crosley told him that he had decided to bring his family to Washington and he was looking for a place to live. Hiss said he offered to sublet the apartment to Crosley. "My recollection is that he spent several nights in my [P Street] house because his furniture had not arrived. We put him and his wife and little baby up two or three nights in a row. It may have been four or five nights. I imagine my wife would testify it seemed even longer than that."

Hiss said he was not prepared at that point in his testimony to say that George Crosley and Whittaker Chambers were one and the same person. But if they were, it might account for Chambers's intimate knowledge of the Hiss family and its homes.

Hiss said that the Crosley family occupied the sublet

apartment through the summer of 1935 but Crosley never paid the promised rent. He described Crosley as a "deadbeat." But before Crosley reneged on the rent agreement, Hiss said, he also turned over to him the old Hiss family automobile—the Ford about which Chambers had previously testified. Hiss said the Crosley family moved out of the sublet apartment when the original lease expired.

HISS: I think I saw him several times after that. I think he told me he moved from here to Baltimore.

NIXON: Even though he didn't pay his rent, you saw him several times?

HISS: He was about to pay it and was going to sell his articles. He gave me a payment on it on account once. He brought a rug over, which he said some wealthy patron gave him. I have still got the damned thing.

NIXON: Did you ever give him anything?

HISS: Never anything but a couple of loans. Never got paid back.

NIXON: Have you ever heard of him since 1935?

HISS: No. Never thought of him again until this morning. . . .

Nixon questioned Hiss about various personal matters concerning the Hiss family that had been mentioned in Chambers's testimony. Hiss's testimony jibed closely with that of Chambers on a number of items. For example, Hiss confirmed that he and his family had owned a cocker spaniel. He also described bird-watching as one of his hobbies.

Nixon told Hiss that Chambers had said he would be willing to take a lie-detector test concerning his testimony, and asked whether Hiss would also take such a test. Hiss said he wanted to obtain further information about the accuracy of lie-detector tests before making a decision. The hearing adjourned for the day with agreement that the next step would be the arrangement of a confrontation between Hiss and Chambers.

The confrontation took place the following day in a sitting room at the Commodore Hotel in New York which had been converted into a temporary hearing room. Once again, the hearing was conducted in secret by Nixon's subcommittee. Members of the subcommittee sat behind a small table that served as a rostrum. When Hiss entered the room, he was instructed to sit in a chair facing the congressmen. To his right was a couch, where Chambers was to sit on his arrival. Nixon told Hiss that the committee wanted to determine whether Whittaker Chambers was the man Hiss had described as George Crosley, and that Chambers had been asked to come to the hotel room so that Hiss could "make up his own mind on that point."

Chambers was waiting in an adjoining room. A committee staff member was sent to get him. As Chambers entered the room, he walked behind Hiss and took a seat on the couch. Hiss did not turn to look at him, but stared straight ahead through a window behind the committee members. Nixon asked Hiss and Chambers to stand.

NIXON: Mr. Hiss, the man standing over there is Whittaker Chambers. I ask you now if you have ever known that man before?

HISS: May I ask him to speak? Will you ask him to say something?

NIXON: Yes. Mr. Chambers, will you tell us your name and your business?

CHAMBERS: My name is Whittaker Chambers.

Hiss stepped toward Chambers, stopped about a foot away from him, looked down at his mouth, and said: "Would you mind opening your mouth wider?" In previous secret testimony, Hiss had said that George Crosley had "bad teeth." He apparently wanted Chambers to open his mouth wider so that he could look more closely at his teeth. He then asked to have Chambers talk a little more.

Nixon handed Chambers a magazine and asked him to read from it. After listening briefly, Hiss said: "I think he is George Crosley, but I would like to hear him talk a little longer. Are you George Crosley?"

Chambers replied: "Not to my knowledge. You are Alger Hiss, I believe."

"I certainly am."

Chambers said: "That was my recollection."

Hiss said that he thought "considerable dental work" had been done, and that he was not willing to "take an absolute oath that he must be George Crosley."

Nixon asked Chambers whether his teeth had undergone any extensive dental work since 1934. Chambers said several of his teeth had been pulled and some bridgework had been installed. Hiss said he would like to have the original condition of Chambers's teeth verified by the dentist who had done the work.

Nixon, Counsel Stripling, and Hiss continued at length on the question of the teeth as the only means of identifying a man who had stayed at Hiss's house, received his old car, and with whom he had had a number of meetings.

Chambers was again questioned about whether he had ever used the name George Crosley, what his relationship to Hiss had been, and whether they had both been communists at the time. The questioning returned to the point

[116]

of Chambers's testimony that he had stayed at the Hiss apartment.

It was at that point that the investigation took another abrupt twist. Without offering any explanation, Hiss suddenly declared: "Mr. Chairman, I don't need to ask Mr. Whittaker Chambers any more questions. I am now perfectly prepared to identify this man as George Crosley."

STRIPLING: You identify him positively?

HISS: I will, on the basis of what he has just said, positively identify him without further questioning as George Crosley.

NIXON: Mr. Hiss, another point. Mr. Chambers said he was a communist and you were a communist.

HISS: I heard him.

NIXON: Did you ever have any idea he might be a communist?

HISS: I certainly did not. . . .

MCDOWELL: You positively identify—

HISS: Positively, on the basis of his own statement that he was in my apartment at the time when I say he was there. I have no further question at all. Even if he had lost both his eyes and taken off his nose, I would be sure.

MCDOWELL: Mr. Chambers, is this the Alger Hiss who was also a member of the Communist Party and at whose home you stayed? You make the identification positive?

CHAMBERS: Positive identification.

(Hiss jumped from his chair, stepped toward Chambers, shook his fist at him, and shouted:)

HISS: May I say for the record at this point that I would like to invite Mr. Whittaker Chambers to

[117]

make those same statements out of the presence of this committee, without their being privileged for suit for libel. I challenge you to do it, and I hope you will do it damned quickly.

(Hiss here referred to the fact that statements made before legislative bodies, including congressional committees, cannot be used as the basis for libel or slander suits. But the same statements can provide the substance for such lawsuits if made elsewhere.)

Committee Investigator Louis Russell, fearing Hiss might strike Chambers, tapped Hiss on the shoulder and asked him to sit down. Hiss refused until ordered to do so by the committee. Before returning to his seat, he shouted at Chambers: "You know who started this!"

After the hearing had been adjourned, members of the subcommittee met privately to discuss what to tell the public and press about the secret confrontation between Hiss and Chambers. The discussion resulted in release of a statement that said: "In executive session of the subcommittee . . . it was unanimously determined from the testimony that Mr. Alger Hiss definitely recognized Whittaker Chambers as the person whom he knew as George Crosley during the fall of 1934 to the fall of 1935." The statement announced a meeting of the full committee in public session, with both Hiss and Chambers as witnesses.

But before that public meeting between Hiss and Chambers, there would be several other developments. The committee, while it had established that the two men had known each other, was still confronted with major conflicts in their testimony. It continued seeking additional witnesses who could provide further clues to the true relationship between the men.

The day after the hotel-room confrontation, Hiss's wife appeared in the same room for questioning by Nixon (who was serving temporarily as a one-man subcommittee). She generally supported the story told by her husband about the man known as George Crosley. That same day, Hiss rejected the suggestion that he take a lie-detector test on the basis that federal courts and scientists had "no confidence in any [such] mechanical device thus far developed."

Meanwhile, committee investigators were trying to track down records concerning the old Ford automobile once owned by Hiss. In the files of the District of Columbia Department of Motor Vehicles, they eventually discovered an automobile transfer certificate dated July 23, 1936.

On August 25, the public confrontation between Hiss and Chambers was played out in Washington. Chairman Thomas opened the proceedings by explaining the direct conflict in the testimony of the two men: "As a result of today's hearing, certainly one of these witnesses will be tried for perjury. The Congress and the American people are entitled to the truth."

The testimony in the public hearing covered much the same ground as the closed hearings and the executive sessions. However, Nixon went even more deeply than Mundt in recalling what he contended were inconsistencies in Hiss's story about the car. At various times, he said, Hiss had testified that he had "thrown the car in with the apartment" or "sold Crosley the car" or "given him the car" or "given him the use of it."

It may seem, in retrospect, that the committee spent an uncommon length of time questioning Hiss and other witnesses about the automobile. But at that point, the car was one of the few issues on which the committee had any

[119]

documentary evidence to use in testing the conflicting stories told by Hiss and Chambers. As Nixon told Hiss:

> You are an attorney. I think you are aware of the standard instruction given to a jury in cases involving credibility of witnesses. That instruction is that, if a witness is found to be telling an untruth on any material question, his credibility on other questions is also suspect. That is the purpose of this questioning now.

The committee turned to another conflict in the testimony. Hiss claimed he had last seen Crosley in 1935, but Chambers insisted that he and Hiss had continued their acquaintanceship until 1938. Nixon cross-examined Hiss at length on this point.

Hiss finally requested and received permission to read into the record a letter he had written to the committee, defending himself against Chambers's charges. He reviewed in the letter his long career in government service. He provided the committee with a long list of prominent officials with whom he had worked. "These men are . . . best able to testify concerning the loyalty with which I performed the duties assigned me," he wrote. Hiss then concluded his statement:

> One personal word. My action in being kind to Crosley years ago was one of humaneness, with results which surely some members of the committee have experienced. You do a favor for a man, he comes for another, he gets a third favor from you. When you finally realize he is an inveterate repeater, you get rid of him. If your loss is only a loss of time and money, you are lucky. You may find yourself calumniated in

a degree depending on whether the man is unbalanced or worse.

The letter and Hiss's testimony failed to convince at least several members of the committee that he was telling the truth. Congressman Hébert, for example, accused Hiss of "hedging" and "resorting to every technicality" in his testimony. Congressman Mundt said that Hiss's initial testimony had been "very persuasive and convincing" but his later testimony had created many doubts.

When the committee finished questioning Hiss at the hearing, Chambers took the witness chair and repeated the charges he had previously made. He was then asked for his reaction to Hiss's testimony. "Mr. Hiss is lying," Chambers said. Hébert asked if he meant that Hiss's account was "pure fabrication out of the whole cloth." Chambers replied: "I would say it is at least eighty percent fabrication."

When the hearing ended, the committee seemed near a dead end in its investigation. Although doubt had been cast on Hiss's credibility, the committee had failed to prove conclusively who was telling the truth. But before the committee made a final decision on the matter, fresh events contrived to change the situation.

Two days after the public confrontation, Chambers made an appearance on the "Meet the Press" radio program. One of his interviewers, reporter Edward Folliard of the *Washington Post*, asked: "Are you willing to say now that Alger Hiss is or ever was a communist?"

Chambers answered: "Alger Hiss was a communist and may be now."

"Does that mean that you are now prepared to go into court and answer to a suit for slander or libel?"

"I do not think Mr. Hiss will sue me for libel."

Chambers was wrong. A month after the broadcast, Hiss sued him for $50,000—later raised to $75,000. The case was filed in federal district court in Baltimore, whose jurisdiction over the suit was based on the fact that the "Meet the Press" broadcast had originated in Maryland and Chambers lived in the state.

As is customary in such cases, pretrial proceedings were conducted. Attorneys for both sides took sworn statements —called depositions—from Chambers, Hiss, and other potential witnesses. In questioning Chambers at one of the deposition hearings, a lawyer who represented Hiss, William Marbury, tried to shake Chambers's story by pointing out that he had produced no documentary evidence to support his version of his dealings with Hiss. Surely, Marbury said, Chambers would have some proof if his story were true. And Chambers did not have any such documentary evidence, did he?

In response, Chambers reached into his jacket pocket and pulled out a thick bundle of documents. He threw them dramatically on a table in front of him. "Only these," he said. "Alger Hiss gave me these when we worked together in the communist conspiracy."

The bundle contained typewritten copies of forty-four documents removed from State Department files during early 1938, plus longhand notes concerning other documents. Chambers said that Hiss, while working in the State Department, had repeatedly smuggled copies of secret documents to him and he had turned them over to communist agents. Shortly before quitting the Communist Party, he said, he had deliberately kept these documents to serve as what he called his "life preserver." In case the communists threatened him or his family because of his break with the party, Chambers said, he intended to use them as a means of gaining bargaining power.

Chambers's disclosure of the existence of the documents, and his account of how they had come into his possession, represented an admission that he had lied in his previous testimony to the Un-American Activities Committee. In that testimony, he had denied that the Washington communist group to which he belonged had been involved in espionage. He had said its purpose had been strictly to place communists in positions where they could influence government policy.

Asked by Marbury to explain why he had not told this version earlier, Chambers replied: "From the beginning, I have faced two problems. My first problem was to paralyze and destroy, in so far as I was able, the communist conspiracy. My second problem was to do no more injury than necessary to the individuals involved in that operation." But he had become angered, he said, over what he considered unfair tactics used by the Hiss forces in the libel case. Chambers felt, for one thing, that his wife, Esther, had been subjected to unduly harsh questioning by Hiss's lawyers during the pretrial proceedings. For another thing, he claimed supporters of Hiss had been spreading malicious rumors that he was insane or an alcoholic. As a result, he said, he had decided to consider making use of the old documents. Chambers gave an account of the storage of the documents in an unused dumb-waiter in Brooklyn and their subsequent retrieval.

Chambers told Marbury that he had brought the documents to the attention of his attorneys but he had initially been unable to decide whether to use them as evidence in the libel case. "My counsel very strongly urged that I had practically no other choice," he said. "The result of my

[123]

turmoil—which is merely the last act of the turmoil that has been going on for a decade—was the decision to give you [Marbury] the material."

The attorneys for Hiss and Chambers felt the documents were sufficiently important that they took them to Federal Judge W. Calvin Chesnut who had been assigned to preside over the libel case. A telephone call was then placed to Alex Campbell, chief of the Justice Department's Criminal Division, who hurried to Baltimore to look over the documents. Agreeing that the documents were extremely important, Campbell took custody of them and returned to Washington—warning all concerned to say nothing to anyone else about the matter.

Nonetheless, rumors began circulating that there had been a startling new development in the Hiss-Chambers affair. The rumors reached, among others, members of the House Un-American Activities Committee. Congressman Nixon and Counsel Stripling decided to drive to Chambers's farm home at Westminster, Maryland, to see what they could learn.

When they arrived, Chambers quickly blurted out the story about the documents, and how they had been taken back to Washington by Campbell. "Before he left he warned everybody present to say nothing whatever . . . if we did divulge any information, we would be guilty of contempt of court," Chambers said. "So I can't tell you what was in the documents. I will only say that they were a real bombshell."

Nixon feared that the Justice Department, which was under the control of President Truman's Democratic administration, might whitewash the affair in an attempt to spare the Democrats embarrassment—and also, President

Truman had been highly critical of HUAC's investigation of the case.

Nixon asked Chambers: "Do you mean that Campbell has these documents in his possession and it is completely up to him if anything is done about them?"

"No, I wouldn't be that foolish," Chambers replied. "My attorney has photostatic copies, and also I didn't turn over everything I had. I have another bombshell in case they try to suppress this one."

"You keep that second bombshell," Nixon told him. "Don't give it to anybody except the committee." Chambers made no commitment, and Nixon and Stripling returned to Washington.

Nixon was planning to leave the next day on a vacation cruise to the Panama Canal Zone. Before doing so, however, he stopped off at the committee office and signed a subpoena calling on Chambers to turn over to the committee any documents still in his possession that bore on the Hiss case. The following day, two committee investigators, William Wheeler and Donald Appell, met Chambers in Washington and served the subpoena on him. The three men then drove to Chambers's farm, arriving about 10 P.M. What followed resembled a scene straight out of a spy movie.

Chambers walked into a pumpkin patch on his farm, then bent over and seemed to be looking for something. He returned and told Wheeler and Appell he had been unable to find what he was seeking. He walked into his house and turned on some lights that beamed into the pumpkin patch. Walking back into the patch, he picked up a pumpkin, looked it over, then put it back on the ground. Next, he picked up another pumpkin. This one had been hol-

[125]

lowed out, in the manner of a Hallowe'en pumpkin, and the top had been put back in place.

Chambers removed the top and reached inside. He pulled out five rolls of microfilm, handed them to the committee investigators, and put the pumpkin back on the ground.

This cache of evidence came to be known as the "pumpkin papers." Many persons assumed the microfilm had been hidden inside the pumpkin for years. Actually, it had been thus concealed for only one day. Originally, the microfilm had been hidden with the other documents in the envelope stashed in the Brooklyn dumb-waiter. When Chambers retrieved the envelope, he removed the microfilm and hid it in his home while turning the other documents over to the lawyers in the libel case. Then, on the day before Wheeler and Appell came to his farm, Chambers saw several private investigators working for Hiss approach his property. Fearing that they might try to search his home, Chambers hid the microfilm inside the pumpkin.

When the contents of the microfilm were revealed to committee members, they turned out to bear copies of still other secret State Department documents. Congressman Mundt issued a statement that concluded: "These microfilms [secured by subpoena from Whittaker Chambers] have been the object of a ten-year search by agents of the United States government and provide definite proof of one of the most extensive espionage rings in the history of the United States."

Word of the recovery of the microfilm was radioed to Nixon. A Coast Guard seaplane was sent to rendezvous with his ship at sea and fly him back to Washington. He arrived to find a struggle in progress between the committee and the Justice Department over use of the recovered documents.

Justice Department attorneys began presenting evidence to a federal grand jury, based on the initial batch of recovered documents. They demanded that the committee also turn over the recovered microfilm. Committee members—claiming they still feared a whitewash by the department—refused to surrender the microfilm and announced plans to conduct new hearings. The Justice Department contended that such hearings might interfere with the grand jury investigation. It said Chambers was under subpoena to testify before the grand jury, and therefore could not be called as a witness at the committee hearings.

The dispute ended with a compromise. Members of the committee agreed to furnish the Justice Department with enlarged copies of the documents that appeared on the microfilm. And the department agreed to allow the committee to question Chambers.

When Chambers appeared before the committee, he testified that Hiss and other government officials with whom he had dealt, had smuggled secret documents to him for several years. Hiss, he said, usually took the documents with him overnight: Sometimes he turned the documents themselves over to Chambers—who got them microfilmed by fellow communists; Chambers then returned the documents to Hiss in time to be replaced in the State Department files the next morning. At other times, Hiss's wife made typewritten copies of the documents on the family's Woodstock typewriter. These copies were then given to Chambers. The microfilmed or typewritten copies were passed by Chambers to his communist superiors—

most often a Soviet intelligence agent named Colonel Boris Bykov. He said Bykov then channeled the documents to Moscow. Chambers gave the same account to the grand jury.

Hiss, appearing before both the committee and the grand jury, adamantly denied turning any State Department documents over to Chambers. Of course, the fact that Chambers had been able to produce the documents did not prove that he had obtained them from Hiss. FBI agents began looking for evidence that would support or rebut Chambers's story.

They tried, without success, to find the Woodstock typewriter formerly owned by the Hiss family. The agents hoped to match typing from the old typewriter with that on Chambers's typewritten documents. They eventually found two letters apparently typed by Mrs. Hiss on the Woodstock. Government experts compared the typing on those letters and on Chambers's documents and said both had been produced by the same machine. In addition, some of the longhand notes included in Chambers's documents were identified by handwriting specialists as being in Hiss's writing.

This evidence was presented to the federal grand jury, although it actually had no power to indict anyone on espionage charges. Under both state and federal law, most crimes (with the chief exception being murder) are subject to the statute of limitations. The statute provides that persons accused of crimes must be prosecuted within a specific period, usually no more than seven years, after the commission of the offenses. After the statute of limitations expires, they are immune from prosecution. In the Hiss case, the statute had clearly expired on any alleged acts of espionage.

However, if the government lawyers could produce evidence showing that Hiss lied when being questioned by the grand jury, they could get him indicted on perjury charges. The alleged perjury would be a fresh offense and would thus not be barred by the statute of limitations.

In questioning Hiss before the grand jury, Assistant Attorney General Thomas J. Donegan asked if he had ever turned over State Department documents, or copies of such documents, to Whittaker Chambers. He also asked if Hiss could definitely say that he had not seen Chambers after January 1, 1937. Hiss replied that he had never turned over any such documents, nor had he seen Chambers after that date.

The grand jurors concluded that Hiss had lied in both answers. On December 15, 1948, they indicted him on two counts of perjury. The indictment charged that, contrary to his testimony, Hiss delivered to Chambers "copies of numerous secret, confidential and restricted documents, writings, notes and other papers" in February and March of 1938. Although Chambers admitted he had lied at least a half-dozen times in his original testimony before the Un-American Activities Committee—when he denied he and Hiss had been engaged in espionage activities—he was not indicted.

Hiss went on trial on the perjury charges on May 31, 1949. The trial ended in a hung jury, with eight jurors voting for conviction and four for acquittal. A second trial began on November 17, 1949. Much of the testimony centered on expert witnesses' contention that many of the copied documents had been typed on the typewriter formerly owned by Hiss. Hiss's lawyers, who had managed to trace the typewriter and produce it in court, offered several theories in attempts to rebut the charge of perjury.

One theory was that Chambers somehow could have gained access to the typewriter while it was in Hiss's possession and typed the documents himself. Another was that Chambers or the FBI could have committed "forgery by typewriter" by altering another machine to make it produce typing characteristics identical to those of Hiss's old Woodstock.

Such theories did not convince the jurors. On January 21, 1950, they found Hiss guilty on both perjury counts. Federal District Judge Henry W. Goddard sentenced him to serve five years in prison. Hiss's lawyers appealed the conviction all the way to the U.S. Supreme Court, but lost. Meanwhile, Hiss's libel and slander suit against Chambers was dismissed.

On March 22, 1951, Hiss entered the Lewisburg Federal Prison in Pennsylvania. He served three years and eight months before being released, with time off for good behavior, in November 1954. After his release, he became a salesman of printing supplies in New York. Over the years, he has made repeated efforts to clear his name.

During 1975, Hiss won what he regarded as two partial victories in his campaign. In one, the Supreme Judicial Court in Massachusetts—where he had first practiced law but had later been stripped of his attorney's license because of the perjury conviction—ruled that he should be given the right to resume practice in the state. The court did not consider whether Hiss had been innocent or guilty in the perjury case, but found that he had demonstrated "moral and intellectual fitness" since his release from prison and therefore was entitled to have his attorney's license reinstated. Hiss, then seventy years of age, immediately took the oath of admission to the Massachusetts bar but said he would spend only part of his time practicing law—meanwhile continuing to sell printing supplies in New York. In the second development that he found encouraging, the U.S. Justice Department agreed to make public some long-secret documents relating to his perjury case—the "pumpkin papers." Hiss contended the documents would help prove his innocence, but that remains to be seen at this writing.

As for Whittaker Chambers, he resigned his job at *Time* magazine and retired to his Maryland farm during the furor over the Hiss case. On July 9, 1961, at the age of sixty, Chambers died.

Controversy continues to rage in some circles today over the Hiss–Chambers affair. Some argue that the facts clearly proved Hiss's guilt. Supporters of Hiss claim that he was innocent and evidence was concocted to frame him. They contend he was the victim of one of the most flagrant political witch hunts in the nation's history.

No matter which view is correct, it remains obvious that the Hiss case played a major role in the history of American witch hunts. Members and supporters of HUAC and other organizations that claimed to be fighting "subversion" in government used the jury's verdict in the Hiss case in attempts to justify all manner of witch hunts of the past and future. They said, in effect: "You see, we've been right all along."

Such arguments led inexorably to extensive new witch hunts. Fresh waves of political hysteria swept across the country. Amid such turmoil, the nation became ripe for the era of McCarthyism.

SOURCES AND SUPPLEMENTARY READING

Walter Goodman's *The Committee* sets in perspective the background from which the drama of the Alger Hiss case emerged.

Countless newspaper and magazine articles have been written about the case, as have a considerable number of books. Much of my material for this chapter was taken from testimony before the House Un-American Activities Committee and trial courts. Both Richard M. Nixon's book, *Six Crises* (Doubleday, 1962), and *A Tragedy of History* by Bert and Peter Andrews (Robert B. Luce, Inc., 1962) draw heavily on such testimony in attempts to explain the case. Since Nixon was an active participant in the investigation and initially came to national attention as a supposed "exposer" of Hiss, *Six Crises* could hardly be expected to be a dispassionate account. It is, nonetheless, valuable in helping a reader explore Nixon's thinking on the threat of subversion—a subject he would use years later to help justify the Watergate affair. Bert Andrews died before completing his account of the Hiss case, in which he played a role as a leading Washington journalist who befriended Nixon and cooperated with him during the committee investigation. His son, Peter, completed the book. And although it occasionally betrays the authors' own biases, it is generally fair and informative.

Hiss and Chambers also wrote books involving the case. *In the Court of Public Opinion* (Alfred A. Knopf, 1957) constitutes an attempt by Hiss to convince readers of his innocence in spite of a jury's guilty verdict. *Witness* (Random House, 1952) is an autobiography that tells Chambers's version of the story. Both books, by their very nature, are biased, but both are enlightening.

9
★ ★ ★
Joe McCarthy
Discovers Subversion

It was just two weeks after Alger Hiss's conviction in the perjury trial that Senator Joseph R. McCarthy, Republican of Wisconsin, publicly adopted the issue of alleged subversion in government. On February 9, 1950, McCarthy appeared in Wheeling, West Virginia, to deliver a speech before a Republican women's organization. After making some preliminary remarks about the dangers of communism, McCarthy dramatically declared:

> While I cannot take the time to name all the men in the State Department who have been named as members of the Communist Party and members of a spy ring, I have here in my hand a list of 205 that were known to the secretary of state as being members of the Communist Party and who, nevertheless, are still working and shaping policy in the State Department.

[133]

Actually, McCarthy had no such thing in his hand. As he would later concede, what he held in his hand at the time was "an old laundry list." But the speech in Wheeling placed him on a path that would eventually lead him to become the most controversial congressional witch hunter in the nation's history.

Until that time, McCarthy had put together a colorful but relatively undistinguished career. Born on November 14, 1908, in Grand Chute Township, Wisconsin, he left school at the age of fourteen to work on his father's farm. At twenty, he decided he would need an education and returned to school—completing a four-year high school course in one year. He then entered Marquette University. In his senior year, he ran for class president against a student named Charles Curran, who had previously beaten him in an election for the presidency of the debating society. During the campaign for the class presidency, McCarthy and Curran each pledged publicly to vote for the other. The election ended in a tie. Curran proposed that they cut a deck of cards to determine the winner, but McCarthy insisted on having another vote a week later. The second election resulted in McCarthy's winning by two votes—indicating that only one student had changed his vote. Curran, infuriated, asked McCarthy: "Joe, did you vote for yourself?" McCarthy replied: "Sure. You wanted the best man to win, didn't you?"

The incident was characteristic of McCarthy's behavior. He hated to lose at anything, no matter what had to be done to avoid it. Originally intending to become an engineer, McCarthy changed his mind while at Marquette and switched to the study of law. He received his law degree in 1935 and immediately hung out his shingle in the small county-seat town of Waupaca, Wisconsin. His

[134]

practice there lasted nine months, during which he handled only four cases and supported himself chiefly by playing poker at a roadside tavern.

Then a veteran attorney with a thriving practice, Mike G. Eberlein, invited McCarthy to join his firm in the nearby town of Shawano. McCarthy accepted and, once there, began joining numerous civic, social, and religious organizations—anxious to meet as many persons as possible because he had already decided he would seek public office. He also became active in politics. In the fall of 1936, despite his recent arrival in Shawano, he ran for district attorney and finished second in a three-man race.

His law partner, Eberlein, had long been a fixture in local political and civic activities. He felt that, because of his many years of service, he should be rewarded with a circuit court judgeship that was up for election in 1939. When Eberlein told McCarthy that he planned to run for the post, McCarthy encouraged him—saying he would make a great judge. The next thing Eberlein knew, McCarthy himself suddenly entered the race for the same judgeship. Eberlein, believing McCarthy had chosen an odd way to show his gratitude for being taken into a prosperous law practice, asked him to leave the firm. McCarthy did so, and embarked on an energetic campaign.

Spending as many as twenty hours a day on the stump, McCarthy tried to visit every farm in the three-county judicial district. He inquired about the crops, tasted housewives' pies, kissed babies—anything that he thought would help attract votes. Although his opponents ridiculed his lack of experience and called him unqualified for the bench, they could not help but envy the vigor with which he threw himself into the campaign. On election day, McCarthy emerged as the surprise winner. At the age of thirty, he became the youngest circuit court judge in the state.

McCarthy worked hard as a judge, clearing up a large backlog of cases, but was reprimanded several times by higher courts for the arbitrary manner in which he sometimes dispensed justice. Once, for example, McCarthy dismissed a case filed by the State Agriculture Department that accused a large dairy firm of using pricing practices that discriminated against small farmers. When state officials appealed McCarthy's decision to the State Supreme Court, the higher court asked for the stenographic transcript of the proceedings conducted in McCarthy's court. There was no such transcript; McCarthy said he had ordered his stenographer to destroy her notes on the case because they were irrelevant. The Supreme Court sharply criticized McCarthy, calling his action "highly improper" and "an abuse of judicial power." It said that "the destruction of evidence under these circumstances could only be open to the inference that the evidence destroyed contained statements of fact contrary to the position taken by the person destroying the evidence." McCarthy's decision was reversed.

Undaunted, McCarthy set his sights on higher office—specifically a seat in the United States Senate. He saw as his chief rival for the next Republican senatorial nomination the newly elected mayor of Milwaukee, Carl Zeidler, a young, handsome man widely regarded as Wisconsin's most promising political figure. When the United States entered World War II, Zeidler enlisted in the navy, and reports of his military exploits received broad publicity throughout the state. McCarthy, as a judge, was exempt from the military draft, and for more than six months took advantage of the exemption. But in June 1942, after deciding that he would need the glamour of a military career in his record if he hoped to win the Senate nomination over Zeidler, McCarthy enlisted in the marines amid great fanfare.

His fellow judges wanted him to resign from the bench, so that another judge could be named to replace him and prevent the development of a backlog of cases. But McCarthy refused, insisting on taking a leave of absence instead. His decision was protested by the chief circuit judge, but was allowed to stand.

Although McCarthy later claimed he had enlisted as "a buck private," he actually asked for and was given a commission as a lieutenant within two days of joining the marines. He subsequently was promoted to captain. After spending almost a year at posts in the United States, McCarthy was shipped to the Pacific war zone. On June 22, 1943, he was aboard the navy ship *Chandeleur* as it steamed from Hawaii toward the New Hebrides Islands. When the ship crossed the equator, crewmen and passengers engaged in the traditional "shellback" ceremony —in which those who had never before crossed the equator were paddled, sprayed with hoses, and subjected to other indignities. McCarthy, one of those being hazed, was descending from a ladder with a bucket tied to one foot when he slipped and fell, breaking three bones in his leg. This was the only injury McCarthy suffered while in service, but he would later claim that he was "a wounded war veteran." During one of his later political rallies, for example, a constituent asked him why he wore shoes

[137]

with built-up heels and soles. "I'll tell you why I wear this shoe," McCarthy said. "It's because I carry ten pounds of shrapnel in this leg."

When he arrived on the New Hebrides island of Espiritu Santo, McCarthy settled into a job as intelligence officer for a marine dive-bomber squadron. It was a desk job, in which his duties involved interviewing pilots returning from bombing missions in order to determine what targets they had hit, what targets remained, and similar information. The dive-bombers had room for only two fliers, the pilot and a tail-gunner. Occasionally, when the pilots did not expect to meet any Japanese resistance, intelligence officers were allowed to ride in the tail-gunners' seats to get an idea of actual flight conditions. McCarthy made several such flights, and never had occasion to fire his machine guns at the enemy. But he delighted in using the guns for target practice at coconut trees on the Pacific islands. Once, he set some kind of record by firing 4,700 practice rounds of ammunition in a single afternoon. Immediately afterward, a large sign was hung on his base. It said: PROTECT OUR COCONUT TREES —SEND MC CARTHY BACK TO WISCONSIN.

McCarthy, meanwhile, was hanging some signs of his own. One, on his tent, read: HEADQUARTERS— MC CARTHY FOR U.S. SENATE. Others, attached to military trucks, simply said: MC CARTHY FOR U.S. SENATE. McCarthy had numerous pictures taken of himself, usually in the tail-gunner's seat of one plane or another, and mailed them to friends back home, who saw that they were published in Wisconsin newspapers. He acquired the nickname "Tail-Gunner Joe," which some said he gave himself, and it found its way into the newspapers. Readers at home had no way of knowing

[138]

that he was far from the hero he painted himself to be.

In 1944, while still in the marines, McCarthy filed as a candidate for the Republican nomination for a Wisconsin seat in the U.S. Senate. He did not have to worry about competition from Carl Zeidler, for the former Milwaukee mayor had been killed when his navy ship had been attacked by a Japanese submarine. But he still faced strong opposition. The incumbent senator, Alexander Wiley, had been endorsed for reelection by the state's leading Republicans.

Several obstacles seemed to be in the path of McCarthy's candidacy. First, military regulations forbade anyone in the armed forces to campaign for public office. Second, since he had refused to resign his office he was still a circuit judge, and the Wisconsin Constitution provided that judges were prohibited from running for any other elected positions. McCarthy simply ignored both prohibitions. He got a thirty-day leave from the marines and went home to make campaign appearances. Appearing in uniform before various groups, he prefaced his remarks by saying that military rules prevented him from discussing campaign issues. Then he would add: "If I were able to speak, here's what I'd say." And he would go on to say, in great detail, what he was supposedly barred from saying.

McCarthy lost the primary by an almost 2 to 1 margin to Senator Wiley, who subsequently won the general election. But the 79,380 votes McCarthy collected throughout the state seemed to encourage his prospects in future elections. He remained in the marines until March 29, 1945. Shortly before his discharge, he was re-elected without opposition to his circuit court judgeship.

While carrying out his judicial duties, McCarthy spent

much of his time traveling around Wisconsin—lining up support for another statewide campaign. In 1946, the other Wisconsin senator, Robert M. LaFollette, Jr., was coming up for reelection. LaFollette had served in the Senate since taking the seat vacated by the death of his father, "Fighting Bob" LaFollette, in 1925. The younger LaFollette and his brother, Philip, who served three terms as governor, had dominated Wisconsin politics for years. Originally Republicans, they had broken away from the party in 1934 and formed the Progressive Party—one of the most successful third-party movements in the nation's history. But by 1946, the Progressive Party had disbanded, and Senator LaFollette planned to seek reelection as a Republican. To do so, he would have to win the Republican primary. But McCarthy had the same idea.

McCarthy threw himself into another whirlwind campaign, dashing around the state to line up support from Republican leaders and from voters. When two other prospective candidates showed signs of getting into the race, McCarthy pressured them to stay out—in one case persuading the hopeful that he had no chance of winning, and in the other threatening to make an issue of the man's recent divorce. Both men's decisions to forgo the campaign left McCarthy and LaFollette in a head-to-head confrontation.

LaFollette, tied up in Washington on Senate business during much of the primary race, conducted a lackluster campaign. McCarthy, in contrast, carried on a colorful one—slashing frequently at LaFollette's record and accusing him of being an "absentee candidate." Curiously, in view of what would happen later, several communist-dominated labor unions threw their support to McCarthy.

(Leaders of the unions had been enraged by a speech in which LaFollette had called for vigilance against communism at home and abroad.) McCarthy, when asked about the backing he was getting from communists, replied: "Communists have the same right to vote as anyone else, don't they?" Of course, they did. But it was not a position he would take later during his days as a witch hunter.

On primary day, McCarthy won by a slender margin of 207,935 votes to LaFollette's 202,539. His Democratic opponent in the general election was Howard McMurray, a political science professor at the University of Wisconsin. Ignoring the fact that he had been supported by communists in the primary, McCarthy based much of his campaign on a charge that McMurray was "communistically inclined." The record did not support the charge. McMurray was a liberal Democrat who had publicly opposed the communists. Once, for example, he had led a drive to withdraw Democratic Party support from a congressional candidate who had been found to be a communist.

When McCarthy first made the charge that he was "communistically inclined," McMurray replied: "I have never heard a responsible citizen—I say a *responsible* citizen—challenge my loyalty as an American before. I am sure my friends and my many students in my political science courses of the past years will not challenge my loyalty. This statement is a little below the belt."

Below the belt or not, McCarthy continued making the charge throughout the campaign. He also took out newspaper advertisements that proclaimed: "Joseph R. McCarthy is 100-per-cent American in thought and deed. No one can say that he believes in any foreign 'isms' that have plagued the Democratic Party throughout their reign. This is America. Let's have Americans in the government."

When the votes were tallied, McCarthy received 620,430 votes to 378,772 for McMurray. Attempts were made to get the election invalidated on the ground that McCarthy had again, as in 1944, violated the Wisconsin Constitution by running for the Senate while still holding office as a judge. But the Wisconsin Supreme Court ruled that, while McCarthy might have violated the Constitution, the state courts had no jurisdiction, because the election involved a federal, rather than a state, office. Thus, at the age of thirty-eight, McCarthy went off to Washington as the junior senator from Wisconsin.

The controversy over his election lingered even after he had taken his Senate seat. Miles McMillin, a Wisconsin lawyer and newspaper editorial writer, filed a complaint against McCarthy with the State Board of Bar Commissioners—accusing him of violating judicial ethics by engaging in the Senate race while still a judge. The bar commissioners studied the evidence, then asked the Wisconsin Supreme Court to disbar McCarthy as a lawyer. The Supreme Court ruled that McCarthy had indeed violated "the terms of the Constitution and laws of the State of Wisconsin and . . . his oath as a circuit judge and as an attorney of law." But it declined to disbar him on the ground that the offense he committed was "in a class by itself, which is not likely to be repeated" (since there seemed no likelihood that McCarthy would again become a judge and then engage in another Senate campaign).

In his first few years in the Senate, McCarthy displayed an unimpressive record. He seemed to jump indiscriminately from issue to issue, never taking the time to study any of them in depth. Moreover, he antagonized various senators by making personal attacks on them in Senate speeches (in violation of the chamber's rules). In a poll taken among Washington newsmen, McCarthy was voted the worst member of the entire Senate.

Still, by early 1950, McCarthy was determined to seek re-election in 1952. He decided he would have to settle on some major issue with which to identify himself, one that could be translated into votes back in Wisconsin. In search of such an issue, McCarthy conferred with three friends over dinner at Washington's fashionable Colony Restaurant on the evening of January 7, 1950. His companions were William A. Roberts, a prominent Washington lawyer; the Reverend Edmund Walsh, dean of Georgetown University's School of Foreign Service; and Charles A. Kraus, a political science instructor at Georgetown.

The four men took turns throwing out ideas on issues that might appeal to McCarthy's constituents. Roberts suggested that McCarthy become a champion of the proposed construction of the St. Lawrence Seaway. But McCarthy vetoed the idea, complaining that it lacked glamour. McCarthy proposed introducing legislation to establish a pension program under which the government would pay $100 a month to every American sixty-five years of age or older. His friends convinced him, however, that the plan was fiscally unsound.

Finally, Father Walsh suggested that McCarthy adopt as his issue the menace of communist subversion. It was a subject in which Father Walsh was deeply interested. He had a long record of staunch anticommunist activities and had written a highly critical book on communism entitled *Total Power*.

[143]

McCarthy immediately agreed that anticommunism would be a powerful issue. Actually, as McCarthy would later concede, he knew almost nothing about communism at the time. But his political instincts told him that the issue could be used expediently in appealing for votes.

Roberts warned that McCarthy could not go off half-cocked—that he would need facts to support any allegations he made. McCarthy said that would be no problem. But actually it did become one—so much so, that Father Walsh, Kraus, and Roberts would shortly wash their hands of McCarthy.

Soon after the dinner meeting at the Colony, McCarthy asked Republican Party officials to line up some speaking engagements for him. In honor of Abraham Lincoln's birthday (February 12), Republicans annually sponsor numerous party dinners throughout the country during the second week in February, and officials assigned McCarthy to speak at several such affairs. He notified them in advance that his subject would be alleged communists in the government. During the 1948 presidential campaign, the Republicans had often accused President Truman of being "soft on communism." Although Truman had won the election in spite of such claims, some Republicans apparently felt in 1950 that the issue was still good for some political mileage. But it is safe to say that nobody—not even McCarthy—had any idea how great an uproar was about to be stirred by the junior senator from Wisconsin.

In preparation for his speaking tour, McCarthy did a smattering of research on communism. But he had only a few rough notes with him when he arrived in Wheeling, West Virginia, on February 9 to deliver the first of his speeches. The local newspaper, the *Wheeling Intelligencer*, reported at length on the speech in which McCarthy claimed to have a list of 205 members of the Communist Party who were working in the State Department. The remark was picked up by the Associated Press and transmitted to newspapers, radio, and television stations throughout the country.

The State Department immediately sent a wire to McCarthy, asking for the 205 names and promising to investigate any information he had. Apparently unnerved by the wire, McCarthy began to backtrack. When he changed planes in Denver, en route to appear on a radio interview program in Salt Lake City on February 10, he found himself surrounded by newsmen and told them that he had been misquoted in Wheeling. He claimed he had not said he knew of 205 communists in the State Department, but rather 205 "security risks" (a term that could include anyone susceptible to blackmail because of alcoholism, marital problems, homosexuality, and the like).

On the Salt Lake City radio program, McCarthy told a third version of the story. Questioned about the Wheeling speech, he said he had not used the figure 205 at all—but instead had charged that he had the names of 57 card-carrying communists working in the State Department. He said that, if Secretary of State Dean Acheson would telephone him, "I will be glad to give him the names of those fifty-seven card-carrying communists."

There was no indication whether Secretary of State Acheson heard of McCarthy's challenge in time to phone him that night. In any event, he did not phone. But a State Department spokesman, Lincoln White, denied that there were any communists in the department: "If we find any, they will be summarily dismissed."

McCarthy flew on to Reno to deliver another speech and played still a fourth version of his numbers game. There, he again used the number 57. He did not claim they were all necessarily card-carrying members of the Communist Party, but were "certainly loyal to the Communist Party [and] nevertheless are still helping to shape our foreign policy." The confusion was compounded by an advance text of the speech McCarthy had distributed to newsmen. The text originally contained the number 205, but that had been scratched out and the number 57 had been substituted for it.

Next, McCarthy sent a telegram to President Truman, challenging the adequacy of government loyalty programs: "I have in my possession the names of fifty-seven communists who are in the State Department at present." He warned Truman in the telegram that the president's failure to provide Congress with a list of communists employed by the department "will label the Democratic Party as being the bedfellow of international communism." Truman did not respond directly to McCarthy, but told a press conference that there was "not a word of truth" in the senator's charges.

The question arose: Just where had McCarthy gotten the figures 205 and 57?

Four years earlier, during a spy scare, rumors had swept Washington that hundreds of communists had somehow infiltrated the State Department. Congressman Adolph Sabath, an Illinois Democrat, asked James F. Byrnes, who was then secretary of state, what the department was doing to prevent such infiltration. Byrnes explained that at the end of World War II about 3,000 employees were transferred to the State Department from other government agencies that had been established to meet the wartime emergency. All 3,000 had been subjected to preliminary security investigations by a departmental screening committee. Of those, the committee had recommended against permanent employment of 284. Seventy-nine of them had been fired at the time, and the remainder were subject to continuing investigations.

McCarthy, as he would later admit, had simply subtracted the figure 79 from 284 and come up with 205—which he had charged were "card-carrying communists" employed in the State Department. Moreover, by the time McCarthy made his charges, only 65 of the 284 persons whose credentials had been questioned were still working for the State Department.

McCarthy used similar methods in coming up with the figure 57. Three years earlier, the House Appropriations Committee conducted an investigation of State Department security procedures. After checking hundreds of the department's personnel files, the committee came up with 108 cases in which it felt there were causes to suspect security problems. In January 1948, the committee began conducting hearings on these cases, each of which was listed only by a code number.

In March 1948, when the State Department prepared a study of the 108 cases under investigation, it showed that only 57 of the persons involved were employed by the department. Of those, 35 had been cleared for continued employment after extensive FBI investigations. The other 22 were still being investigated. In many of the cases, the matters under investigation concerned issues other than alleged subversive activities. McCarthy ignored many of these points and obscured the fact that the information was several years out of date. He simply seized on the figure 57 and continued his ill-founded charges.

When he returned to Washington from his speaking tour, however, no one seemed to know the source for the information on which he had based his allegations. Newsmen were waiting at Washington National Airport to question him. Asked whether he really had a list of communists employed in the State Department, McCarthy at first said he not only had one—but he would show it to the reporters. With that, he reached inside a briefcase and made a show of searching for the list. But he could not find it. He said lamely that he must have left it in his other luggage, and the newsmen did not press him to retrieve the luggage and look for the list.

Meanwhile, Democrats began accusing McCarthy of playing fast and loose with the truth. The Senate majority leader, Scott Lucas of Illinois, charged him with making "shameful" slurs against the State Department. Other Democrats insisted that, if McCarthy really had information about subversion in the department, he should provide names and facts instead of making generalized accusations. McCarthy, enjoying the publicity he was receiving, said he would answer the criticism in a speech on the Senate floor.

When he did take the Senate floor, on February 20, 1950, he touched off one of the most tumultuous spectacles in the chamber's history. From about 6 P.M. until almost midnight, McCarthy engaged in a series of bitter wrangles with Democratic senators as he read into the record a bewildering mass of allegations. Somehow, McCarthy had gotten his hands on a summary of adverse information about the 108 people involved in the House Appropriations Committee's 1948 investigation. Using that and former Secretary of State Byrnes's 1946 information to Congressman Sabath as jumping-off points, McCarthy launched into fresh attacks on the State Department. He concluded that the administration was determined to cover up evidence of alleged subversion. "I do not feel that the Democratic Party has control of the executive branch anymore," he said. "I think a group of twisted-thinking intellectuals has taken over the Democratic Party."

Senator Lucas broke in to challenge McCarthy; he asked the senator to follow through with the speech made at Wheeling: "I want him to name those communists. The senator is privileged to name them all in the Senate, and if these people are not communists he will be protected [against lawsuits]."

McCarthy replied: ". . . I should like to assure [Lucas] that I will not say anything on the Senate floor which I will not say off the floor. On the day when I take advantage of the security we have on the Senate floor, on that day I will resign from the Senate."

McCarthy said it would not be "fair" to identify the people by name. Instead, he planned to read into the record information on 81 cases—identifying the persons only by assigning them numbers. Lucas asked what relation the new figure, 81, had to the previous figures of 205 and 57. McCarthy claimed he had never used the figure 205. He said the 81 cases he would now cite included the 57 mentioned earlier and 24 more: "I am only giving the Senate cases in which it is clear there is a definite communist connection—persons whom I consider to be communists in the State Department."

But he soon began hedging. He admitted, for example, that not all of the 81 persons were still in the State Department. Next, he conceded that not all of them were communists. In fact, he allowed, the information he had on some of the individuals might not be accurate. In

[149]

many instances in which he did charge communist activities, McCarthy made undocumented allegations.

Suspicious of such descriptions, Democratic Senator Brien McMahon of Connecticut interrupted to ask whether McCarthy had the "full files" on the cases he was discussing. McCarthy responded: "The senator asks whether I have the complete State Department files. The answer is 'No.' "

McMahon jumped on that admission. "The senator does not have in his possession any information which will indicate that the derogatory statement is true," he pointed out. But McCarthy said he felt he was giving a fair summary of what was in the files. Then McMahon, who had been a Justice Department lawyer before entering the Senate, told him:

> . . . I call attention to the possibility that, if we had the whole file before us, as undoubtedly the State Department has, the information the senator from Wisconsin is giving the Senate might be contradicted to the point where creditable witnesses or creditable evaluators of the files would say, "In that event, we cannot believe that information."

When McMahon continued prodding McCarthy to provide proof of the truth of his charges, McCarthy replied: "Since when has it been the job of a senator who is a member of the minority . . . to clean house for an executive department? That is the task of the majority, and I hope they take the task on their shoulders."

Republican Senator Kenneth Wherry of Nebraska—trying to bring the evening's confusing events to some logical conclusion—asked whether McCarthy was calling for a Senate investigation of his charges. McCarthy replied that he was. Democratic Leader Lucas promised his party would cooperate in providing McCarthy "a hearing under oath." McCarthy responded that Lucas "thinks this should be a trial of the man digging out the communists and not of the communists themselves."

When the exhausted senators finally adjourned for the night, McCarthy seemed to have won a tactical advantage at least in the publicity department. The debate had been so hectic and complex that journalists could not hope to convey it fully in their published accounts. What most readers got from the news stories was that McCarthy had made sweeping charges of subversion in the State Department and had cited a series of case histories in support of his allegations. It was the old story of denials rating secondary attention to accusations in the press.

The day after the debate, Democratic senators met and decided to try to force a showdown in which McCarthy would be obliged to provide proof of his allegations. Senator Lucas introduced a resolution authorizing a subcommittee of the Senate Foreign Relations Committee to investigate McCarthy's charges. In the debate on the resolution, Lucas insisted that the subcommittee's hearings be open so that the public would ". . . know definitely as soon as possible just who is being charged and who is not being charged with being communists. That is only fair. Every individual in the State Department . . . is under a cloud."

During the debate, McCarthy warned that he would not identify his sources of information—saying that those in the government might be fired if he named them. But Lucas demanded that the committee insist that McCarthy name the sources of his information: "He is responsible for this investigation. He cannot hide behind anonymous informants. His duty, as a senator and as an American, is to tell the committee exactly where he got his information and to name names." McCarthy replied merely that he would cooperate with the investigation.

Lucas's resolution calling for the investigation was passed unanimously by the Senate. Named as chairman of the investigating subcommittee was Democratic Senator Millard E. Tydings of Maryland. The other members were Democrats Brien McMahon of Connecticut and Theodore F. Green of Rhode Island, and Republicans Henry Cabot Lodge, Jr., of Massachusetts and Bourke B. Hickenlooper of Iowa.

Although actually a subcommittee, the investigating group came to be known as the Tydings committee. Chairman Tydings was a conservative Democrat who had served in the Senate for twenty-four years. He was known as an independent man who refused to follow the dictates of party leaders. During President Franklin D. Roosevelt's administration, for example, he had opposed many New Deal policies. In retaliation, Roosevelt had tried to purge him in 1938 by supporting Tydings's opponent in a senatorial primary campaign. But Tydings had won reelection and returned to the Senate with increased prestige. When named to head the subcommittee investigating McCarthy's charges, Tydings pledged that the inquiry would be "neither a witch hunt nor a whitewash." But he emphasized that McCarthy would be expected to prove all the allegations he had made.

The Tydings committee hearings began on March 8, 1950. The hearing room, open to the public and press, was jammed. Bright lights illuminated the scene for television cameras.

McCarthy was the first witness. He had barely begun his opening statement before he got into a wrangle with Tydings. In his speech before the Senate, McCarthy had charged that a "high State Department official" had used pressure to force the rehiring of a department employee fired in 1946 on charges of being a homosexual and a security risk. Tydings demanded that McCarthy name the "high State Department official." McCarthy refused, saying the committee could obtain the name by subpoenaing State Department files. (Actually, McCarthy admitted to newsmen later in the day, he did not even know the official's name.)

Tydings, angered by McCarthy's response, snapped: "You are in the position of being the man who occasioned this hearing, and so far as I am concerned in this committee you are going to get one of the most complete investigations ever given in the history of the Republic."

McCarthy replied that he would submit the information concerning disloyalty and security risks in the State Department, but it was up to the committee to investigate the cases. He adamantly refused to identify his sources of information. He then accused Senator McMahon and the committee of being tools of the State Department.

While standing by his refusal to identify his sources, McCarthy did begin to provide the names of persons he accused of communist activities. The first name he dropped in his testimony was that of a former municipal court judge in New York City, Dorothy Kenyon. He claimed that her case was "extremely important in that it will shed considerable light on the workings of our loyalty program."

Just how it would do that was never explained, for the

fact was that Miss Kenyon had never worked for the State Department.

When Miss Kenyon heard about McCarthy's charges, she called him an "unmitigated liar" and demanded immediate opportunity to answer him before the Tydings committee. "Senator McCarthy comes from Wisconsin, sometimes called the state of great winds," she said. "He is a wonderful example."

The committee promptly called her as a witness, and she adamantly denied all of McCarthy's allegations. Acknowledging that over the years she had joined a great many organizations she believed were pursuing worthy aims, Miss Kenyon said she had withdrawn from a number of them upon learning they had been infiltrated by communists. Although McCarthy had accused her of belonging to twenty-eight communist-front organizations, he had named only twenty-four. Of those, Miss Kenyon testified she had belonged to twelve—none of which had been designated as a communist front while she was a member. She said that she currently belonged to none of the organizations and that many of them had been dissolved years earlier. She concluded her testimony with the words: "There is not a communist bone in my body."

McCarthy did not attend the hearing at which Miss Kenyon testified. But Senator Hickenlooper, who usually served as one of McCarthy's chief Republican supporters, told Miss Kenyon at the conclusion of her testimony he could find not "the least evidence or belief" that she had ever been "in any way subversive or disloyal."

Such a statement—coming from Hickenlooper—should have served as a sharp rebuke to McCarthy. After all, Miss Kenyon's case was the first to be cited by McCarthy. By all logic, if there were any basis to his charges, the first case should have been airtight. Still, McCarthy showed no sign of embarrassment. He launched into a new barrage of allegations.

His next major target was Philip C. Jessup, then serving as U.S. ambassador-at-large. McCarthy charged that Jessup had "an unsual affinity for communist causes" and was "now formulating top-flight policy in the Far East affecting half the civilized world." Jessup was reasonably well known to the American public. He had previously served as United States delegate to the United Nations, where he had received wide publicity for standing up firmly against communist delegates in debates. For his work at the UN, he had been denounced by Soviet propagandists as a "capitalistic warmonger."

Jessup, who had been a professor of international law at Columbia University and had served in several high State Department jobs, was on a twelve-nation tour of the Far East at the time McCarthy made the accusations against him. Curiously, during the same week McCarthy charged him with procommunist sympathies, the Soviet newspaper *Izvestia* accused him of making "slanderous anticommunist" statements in the course of his Asian trip. When he learned of McCarthy's allegations, Jessup flew home and asked to appear before the Tydings committee. He said that examination of his record in public office showed he was a strong anticommunist:

> If Senator McCarthy's innuendoes were true, the representatives of foreign governments with whom I spoke [on the Far East tour] would be entitled to believe that my statements to them were deceitful and fraudulent. . . . It may be relatively unimportant whether the character of a single American citizen is

blackened and his name brought into disrepute, but in the present serious situation of international relations throughout the world today it is a question of the utmost gravity when an official holding the rank of ambassador-at-large of the United States of America is held up before the eyes of the rest of the world as a liar and a traitor.

Jessup then presented the committee with letters he had received from two of the nation's best-known military leaders, retired Army Generals George C. Marshall and Dwight D. Eisenhower, attesting to his loyalty.

In assailing Jessup, McCarthy had based his charges largely on the contention that the ambassador had served as a sponsor of an organization known as the American-Russian Institute. The evidence showed, however, that Jessup had never been a sponsor of the institute itself. He had merely permitted his name to be listed, with those of many other prominent Americans, as a sponsor of two dinners given by the institute—one of them a memorial dinner honoring the late President Roosevelt. Moreover, the first dinner had taken place in 1944, when Russia was a wartime ally of the United States; and the second, in 1946, when the U.S. attorney general's office had specifically excluded the American-Russian Institute from its list of organizations officially designated as subversive.

When Jessup finished his testimony, McCarthy seemed once again to have failed to substantiate his charges. Yet he then made allegations of subversion against several other State Department employees. But after hearing the evidence, a majority of the Tydings committee members were convinced that the employees were loyal Americans. McCarthy thus far had not come close to producing even one documented case involving a "card-carrying communist" in the State Department.

With his credibility waning sharply, McCarthy decided to put all his chips on the line in one major effort to salvage something from the Tydings committee hearings. He told the committee he was prepared to name "the top Russian espionage agent in the United States—a man he said was then connected with the State Department.

After making that bold declaration, McCarthy delayed naming the man he had in mind—milking a maximum of suspense and publicity from the mystery. His strategy touched off wide speculation. Just who was the man on whose case McCarthy was willing to stand or fall? Did such a man really exist? If so, did McCarthy have the goods on him?

Finally, he dropped the name. It was that of Owen Lattimore. Lattimore had served periodically as an unofficial consultant to the State Department and, at the time of McCarthy's charges, was in Afghanistan with a United Nations economic mission.

Most of Lattimore's life had been devoted to studying and trying to solve the problems of the Far East. He had spent his childhood in China—where his father, an American, had taught school. After attending schools in Switzerland and England, he had done graduate work in anthropology at Harvard University. He had then turned to journalism and traveled widely throughout the Orient, writing hundreds of magazine articles and eleven books on the Far East. In 1938, Lattimore was named director of the Walter Hines Page School of International Relations at Johns Hopkins University. About a year before the United States entered World War II, he became an aide to Chinese President Chiang Kai-shek.

Once the United States got into the war, Lattimore returned home and became deputy director of the Office of War Information. His duties took him to China several times during the war, and he kept in close touch with Chiang. But he became increasingly disillusioned by corruption and inefficiency in Chiang's government. After the war, when Chiang's nationalist forces were engaged in a struggle with the Chinese communists for control of the country, Lattimore urged that Chiang try to reach some kind of accommodation with the communists. Chiang refused, but Lattimore's advice was interpreted by some of his critics as helpful to the communists—who eventually took control of the Chinese mainland and drove Chiang to the island of Formosa.

McCarthy seized on such interpretations and blamed Lattimore largely for the "loss" of China to the communists. But such a view seemed undocumented by the facts, and whatever advice Lattimore gave the State Department was on an unofficial basis. He had no desk at the department and no access to department files, as McCarthy contended.

The FBI had an extensive dossier on Lattimore's background, chiefly because he had worked for the government during the war. At President Truman's direction, members of the Tydings committee were allowed to examine FBI summaries of the material in the Lattimore file. And FBI Director J. Edgar Hoover was authorized by the president to testify before the committee. Hoover took the witness chair and said the FBI file contained no evidence to support McCarthy's charges against Lattimore.

[158]

When word of the Washington furor reached Lattimore in Afghanistan, he left for the United States to appear before the Tydings committee. Before departing, he received a cable from the Associated Press in Washington asking him to comment on McCarthy's charges. Lattimore wired the news agency: "McCarthy's rantings pure moonshine. Delighted his whole case rests on me as this means he will fall flat on his face. . . . As he made his way home, he issued fresh denunciations of McCarthy at virtually every stop.

When he reached Washington, newsmen surrounded him at National Airport. Among other statements, Lattimore said: "A Soviet publication recently called me a 'learned lackey of imperialism.' I am advised that at least one of my books has been banned in the Soviet Union."

But before Lattimore could appear before the Tydings committee, he was the main subject of a curious speech delivered by McCarthy on the Senate floor on March 30, 1950. On the one hand, McCarthy backed away from his charge that Lattimore was "the top Russian espionage agent in the United States." On the other hand, McCarthy continued to hammer away at Lattimore. "In view of his position of tremendous power in the State Department as the 'architect' of our Far Eastern policy, the more important aspects of his case deal with his aims and what he advocates—whether his aims are American aims or whether they coincide with the aims of Soviet Russia."

On April 6, Lattimore appeared before the Tydings committee. McCarthy sat just five yards away from him as he testified. Glaring at his adversary, Lattimore flatly denied all of McCarthy's allegations against him. McCarthy, Lattimore said, had violated the responsibility of his office in various ways:

[159]

He has violated it by impairing the effectiveness of the United States government in its relations with its friends and allies, and by making the government of the United States an object of suspicion in the eyes of the anticommunist world and undoubtedly the laughing stock of communist governments. He has violated it by instituting a reign of terror among officials and employees of the United States government, no one of whom can be sure of safety from attack by the machine gun of irresponsible publicity in Joseph McCarthy's hands.

He has, without authorization, used secret documents obtained from government files. He has vilified citizens of the United States and accused them of high crime, without giving them an opportunity to defend themselves. He has refused to submit alleged documentary evidence to a duly constituted committee of the Senate. . . .

He ridiculed McCarthy's statement that he had been the architect of the nation's Far East policy. Lattimore conceded the policy had been a failure, but denied authorship: "The fact is that I have been very little consulted by those who do make policy. . . . I think I can fairly claim—with great regret—that I am the least consulted man of all those who have a public reputation in this country as specialists on the Far East."

In his testimony, Lattimore became the first person to use the term "McCarthyism" to describe smear techniques and reckless character assassination. The term caught on and became part of the American political lexicon.

At the conclusion of the testimony, Tydings made a statement on behalf of his committee and J. Edgar Hoover that, after a thorough study of the complete summary of Lattimore's FBI file, it was the unanimous opinion that he had never been a communist, nor was he ever connected with espionage.

McCarthy, asked by newsmen for comment on Tydings's statement, said: "Either Tydings hasn't seen the files or he is lying. There is no other alternative."

In an attempt to recover the initiative, McCarthy promised to produce a mystery witness who would support his allegations against Lattimore. When the mystery man finally appeared before the Tydings committee on April 10, he turned out to be Louis Budenz—the same former communist who had come to be known as a perennial witness in investigations into communism since 1946. In all that time, he had never mentioned Owen Lattimore's name. But now, with McCarthy searching for corroboration for his charges, Budenz came to his aid.

He testified that while he was a communist he was told by Earl Browder, then head of the American Communist Party, that Lattimore was subject to communist discipline. He said Browder also told him, during the supposed 1937 conversation, that Lattimore was trying to persuade American writers to publish articles saying that the Chinese communists were merely agrarian reformers. Even if Budenz accurately reported the conversation with Browder—which Browder would later deny—the allegations against Lattimore were obviously hearsay. In addition, they were notably vague.

Republican Senator Lodge, disturbed by the fuzziness of the testimony, asked Budenz to provide "a specific instance" when an order from the Communist Party was carried out by Lattimore. Budenz replied that the instruction to picture the Chinese communists as agrarian reformers was "certainly carried out" by somebody, but he could not specify whom, "because I did not hear the detailed report on the matter." Asked why he had never mentioned Lattimore's name before, during the five years he had been testifying about communism, Budenz said he had just not gotten around to it. Lastly, Budenz admitted that he had never laid eyes on Lattimore.

Browder, who had been expelled from the Communist Party in 1946 on charges of deserting to capitalism, later took the witness chair and disputed Budenz's testimony. Another former Communist Party official, Dr. Bella V. Dodd, provided similar testimony. Also called as a witness was retired Army Brigadier General Elliot R. Thorpe, who had served during and after World War II as chief of counterintelligence for General of the Army Douglas MacArthur. He said he had known Lattimore well during the war and had three times investigated Lattimore's loyalty record. Each time, he said, he found no reason to question his loyalty and cleared him to receive "top-secret" information.

After hearing all the testimony in its investigation of McCarthy's charges, the Tydings committee began reviewing the evidence and preparing a written report on its findings. Meanwhile, McCarthy continued making broad-scale allegations of subversion in the State Department.

But he received a sharp setback on June 1 when seven of his fellow Republican senators signed what they called a "Declaration of Conscience" that deplored the sort of tactics he had adopted. Senator Margaret Chase Smith of Maine rose on the Senate floor to present the declaration on behalf of herself and Senators George Aiken of Vermont, Charles Tobey of New Hampshire, Irving Ives of New York, Edward Thye of Minnesota, Wayne Morse of Oregon, and Robert Hendrickson of New Jersey. Senator Smith began:

> I speak as a Republican. I speak as a woman. I speak as a United States senator. I speak as an American. The United States Senate has long enjoyed worldwide respect as the greatest deliberative body in the world. But recently that deliberative character has too often been debased to the level of a forum of hate and character assassination sheltered in the shield of congressional immunity.
>
> It is ironical that we senators can in debate in the Senate directly or indirectly, by any form of words, impute to any American who is not a senator any conduct or motive unworthy or unbecoming an American—and without that non-senator American having any legal redress against us. Yet, if we say the same thing in the Senate about our colleagues, we can be stopped on the grounds of being out of order.

She warned that suspicions raised by McCarthy's allegations were creating "know-nothing, suspect-everything" attitudes throughout the country. "I don't want to see the Republican Party ride to political victory on the Four Horsemen of Calumny—Fear, Ignorance, Bigotry and Smear."

Then, reading from the "Declaration of Conscience" itself, Senator Smith said: "We are Republicans, but we are Americans first. It is as Americans that we express our

[163]

concern with the growing confusion that threatens the security and stability of our country. . . ."

When Senator Smith finished, she was surrounded and congratulated by senators from both parties. McCarthy, who had been seated directly behind her during her speech, stalked angrily out of the chamber. The next day, in a Senate speech of his own, he served notice that the declaration would not deter him:

> Let me make it clear to the administration, to the Senate and to the country that this fight against communism, this attempt to expose and neutralize the efforts of those who are attempting to betray this country, shall not stop—regardless of what any group in this Senate or in the administration may do. I hold myself accountable not only to them, but first to the people of my state and secondly to the people of the nation and thirdly to civilization as a whole.

On July 17, the three Democratic members of the Tydings committee—Senators Tydings, McMahon, and Green—issued a majority report on their investigation that was filled with harsh condemnation of McCarthy. Republican Senators Lodge and Hickenlooper refused to sign the report denouncing their fellow party member. Even without their support, however, the document represented a severe blow; rarely had senators been so vitriolic in criticizing a colleague. In systematic fashion, the document cited case after case in which McCarthy had made accusations against private citizens and government employees, and then been unable to support them.

In accusing McCarthy of perpetrating "a fraud and a hoax," the report concluded that "This has been done without the slightest vestige of respect for even the most elementary rules of evidence or fair play or indeed common decency. Indeed, we have seen an effort not merely to establish guilt by association, but guilt by accusation alone."

Senator Lodge issued a minority report that did not support McCarthy, but rather complained that the committee investigation had been superficial and had failed to pursue various leads. McCarthy, not unexpectedly, had his own complaints about the investigation and the majority report. He charged: "A reading of it by any fair-minded person will indicate the extent to which the subcommittee has gone to protect communists. I can stand up to the smear. I have expected it."

The majority report was accepted by the full Senate Foreign Relations Committee, which directed in a 9 to 2 vote (with Lodge and Hickenlooper casting the negative votes) that the report be transmitted to the Senate. When Tydings presented the report to the Senate, a tumultuous debate ensued. Until that time, McCarthy had generally been operating without organized support from the Republican leadership; the party's leaders in the Senate had refrained from giving his allegations their official blessing. The Tydings committee report had been so severe in its condemnation of McCarthy, however, that many influential Republicans felt it violated the tradition of senatorial courtesy. Accordingly, party leaders decided to throw their weight behind McCarthy in an attempt to prevent the Senate from accepting the Tydings report.

The tone was set by Senator Robert A. Taft of Ohio, acting as a spokesman for the Senate Republican Policy Committee. Calling the Tydings report "derogatory and insulting to Senator McCarthy," Taft said, "the language used by the Democrats about Senator McCarthy was inexcusable."

In the Senate debate on acceptance of the report, Tydings tore into McCarthy anew—accusing him of stooping to the use of "mud, slime and filth"—then said, "I ask the Senate: 'What are you going to do about it?' I leave it up to the Senate's conscience."

McCarthy replied: "Today, Tydings tried to notify the communists in government that they are safe in their positions. However, I want to assure them that they are not safe." Other Republicans spoke in rebuttal to Tydings, and Senator Hickenlooper called the report "a mysterious document, mysteriously conceived."

When the issue finally came to a vote, forty-five senators (all Democrats) voted in favor of accepting the report, and thirty-seven (all Republicans) voted against it. Thus, the criticism of McCarthy contained in the report was given official Senate sanction.

But if anyone thought a decision reached by voting along such partisan lines would lead McCarthy to abandon his witch-hunting tactics, he was badly mistaken. McCarthy was just getting started.

SOURCES AND SUPPLEMENTARY READING

Although I was only seventeen years of age when Senator Joseph McCarthy joined the witch-hunt movement, I had already begun my career as a journalist. Throughout my college years—both as a student editor and a part-time professional newspaperman—I pursued McCarthy's career closely. My *alma mater*, New York University, was one of many American institutions of higher learning caught up in the witch-hunt controversy, as faculty members were called before Senate committees, questioned about their political beliefs and, in some cases, ousted for refusing to testify. After my college graduation, as a full-time newspaperman, I had further occasion to cover the activities of McCarthy and other witch hunters. Thus, much of the material for the period between 1950 and 1964 (when I left the newspaper business to become a full-time author) concerns events I was involved in describing for readers of various daily newspapers—either as a reporter or editor.

Such material has been supplemented by a voluminous file of newspaper and magazine clippings on witch hunts I have accumulated over the years. Papers such as the *New York Times*, the *Washington Post,* and the now-defunct *New York Herald-Tribune* made dedicated efforts to cover the McCarthy story with fairness and objectivity. Unfortunately, as I have pointed out in the text, the limitations of daily journalism are such that a demagogue of McCarthy's ilk has a great publicity advantage over his victims. By the time the press gets around to publishing their denials of allegations—if it publishes them at all— a man such as McCarthy has already made new allegations that receive headline attention. The denials tend to get lost in the shuffle. Although many newspapers have tried in recent years to improve their techniques for coping with such problems, it remains true that denials rarely catch up with accusations in the daily press.

One function a book such as this can perform is to put into long-range perspective complex events that often are distorted in the news media—both printed and broadcast. In trying to achieve this perspective, I have drawn on other books such as Richard H. Rovere's *Senator Joe McCarthy* (Harcourt, Brace, 1959); Fred J. Cook's *The Nightmare Decade*; Charles E. Potter's *Days of Shame*; and Lately Thomas's *When Even Angels Wept*. It should also be noted that some of those I consider witch hunters, such as former McCarthy aide Roy M. Cohn, have written their own accounts of the period. Cohn has written several books, including one titled simply *McCarthy* (New American Library, 1968), that give what I regard as self-serving defenses of McCarthy's investigative practices. Such works, while biased, are nonetheless valuable in helping capture the witch-hunt era.

10
★ ★ ★

The Faked Photograph
and Other Escapades

Despite the strong criticism leveled at him in the Tydings committee report and elsewhere, Senator Joseph McCarthy increased in popularity among many Americans. Across the country, countless citizens harbored such fears about communism—real or imagined—that they saw the government as virtually bursting with subversives. Many of them viewed Senator McCarthy as the only savior who could prevent a complete communist takeover of the nation. They accepted uncritically McCarthy's claims that those who attacked him were simply trying to cover up the supposedly rampant subversion in government.

Such supporters of McCarthy deluged him with letters, telegrams, phone calls, and personal visits—pledging him various forms of aid. Many sent him money to help in his "crusade." Meanwhile, McCarthy became friendly with some of the country's most wealthy, politically conservative businessmen—including several Texas oil millionaires —who also provided financial help. McCarthy used such private support to hire employees, in addition to his regular complement of government-paid Senate staffers, who could be used in further investigations of alleged subversion.

He also employed his staff and financial resources in attempts to gain revenge against those he regarded as his enemies. Heading his list of targets was Senator Millard Tydings. Within months after completing his work on the committee investigation of McCarthy's charges, Tydings was coming up for reelection to a fifth term in his Maryland Senate seat. In September 1950, he won a Democratic primary by a 3 to 1 margin, and many observers assumed he would win with equal ease in the November general election. But McCarthy, with the help of his staffers and financial backers, decided to take a direct hand in bringing about Tydings's defeat.

The Republican nominee for Tydings's seat was a Baltimore lawyer named John Marshall Butler, who had never before run for public office and was almost unknown among the electorate. McCarthy volunteered to remedy the situation by making speeches on Butler's behalf, devising campaign strategy, assigning staff members to work with the candidate, and rounding up campaign funds from his wealthy contributors. He enlisted the backing of, among others, Mrs. Ruth McCormick Miller, publisher of the *Washington Times-Herald*. Mrs. Miller, in turn, suggested that a Chicago public-relations man, Jon M. Jonkel, be hired to manage Butler's campaign. Maryland law prohibited candidates from hiring campaign managers from outside the state. But at McCarthy's insistence, Butler hired Jonkel anyway—keeping a Maryland man as campaign manager in name only and allowing Jonkel (with the title of "adviser") to make most of the major decisions on campaign operations.

The theme of Butler's campaign, also adopted under pressure from McCarthy, was that Senator Tydings was soft on communism. A key ingredient of the campaign, suggested by McCarthy, was the publication of a four-page tabloid newspaper purporting to give "the facts" about Tydings's political record. The paper was filled with articles that smeared Tydings with false claims of procommunist sympathies. The most flagrant entry in the newspaper was a photograph that appeared to show former Communist Party leader Earl Browder whispering confidentially into Tydings's ear. The photograph was a fake: separate pictures of Tydings and Browder had been taken from newspaper files, and skillfully cut and pasted together by a campaign worker.

McCarthy's research assistant, Jean Kerr (later to become his wife), had been assigned to work on the Butler campaign and had helped prepare the tabloid newspaper. When complaints were raised about use of the fake picture, she insisted she could see nothing wrong with it. The picture "was the type of literature that should go out in a campaign," she said. "The voters should be told what is going on and this certainly did it."

Mrs. Miller ordered 500,000 copies of the campaign newspaper printed on the presses of the *Washington Times-Herald*. The Butler campaign organization hired a Baltimore printer named William Fedder to perform two other chores, and Fedder eventually became involved in a bizarre episode that was to haunt McCarthy and his cohorts. One of Fedder's campaign assignments was to handle folding, addressing, and distribution of the tabloid newspaper. Another was to hire groups of women to sign Butler's name to thousands of hand-written post cards mailed to Maryland voters—making it appear that Butler himself had written the cards.

Fedder was laying out money to pay the women, but had not been paid in full by the campaign organization. He asked Butler to give him a letter promising that he would eventually receive full payment. Butler complied with a letter, apparently not realizing at the time that his letter amounted to an admission that Maryland's election law had been violated. The law limited each candidate in a Maryland election to campaign spending of $5,000. But Butler's debt to Fedder alone—not to mention other campaign expenditures—was $11,000.

McCarthy and his subordinates belatedly learned about the letter's existence, and decided to try to retrieve it from Fedder. Eventually, shortly after midnight, Fedder was summoned to a meeting in Baltimore with McCarthy's chief investigator, Don Surine (who had previously been kicked out of the FBI), and two other McCarthy aides. Fedder later said that Surine demanded the return of the Butler letter but he refused to hand it over. Surine then threatened to make Fedder the target of a McCarthy investigation unless he surrendered the letter; Fedder told him that he did not have the letter—it was in the hands of his attorney. Surine and the two other men responded by forcing him into a car and making him accompany them on an aimless ride through the Baltimore suburbs that lasted for several hours, he said. Finally, under duress, he signed a statement presented to him by Surine that said Butler did not owe him any money. Only then, he said, was he released and permitted to return home.

In the November general election, Butler scored an upset victory over Tydings—defeating him by more than

40,000 votes. The result, in addition to providing Mc-
Carthy the vengeance he had sought against Tydings,
seemed a clear demonstration of his political clout. And
it was not an isolated event. In other states, various candidates for whom McCarthy had also campaigned won
impressive victories. In Illinois, Senate Majority Leader
Scott Lucas—a persistent adversary of McCarthy—was
defeated for reelection by Congressman Everett M. Dirksen. Republican senatorial candidates supported by Mc-
Carthy were elected in Utah and Idaho, while incumbent
Democratic Senators Claude Pepper of Florida and Frank
Graham of North Carolina were defeated in reelection
campaigns opposed by McCarthy.

As a result of the tactics used in the Maryland campaign, Tydings asked for a Senate investigation, which
an elections subcommittee of the Senate Rules Committee
was instructed to carry out. The subcommittee was headed
by Democratic Senator Guy Gillette of Iowa and also
included Democrats Thomas Hennings of Missouri and
A. S. (Mike) Monroney of Oklahoma, and Republicans
Margaret Chase Smith of Maine and Robert Hendrickson
of New Jersey.

By the time Tydings testified before the subcommittee in
early 1951, he appeared as a private citizen who had no
further political ambitions, but who felt compelled to
"disclose certain scandalous, scurrilous, libelous and unlawful practices" used against him in the campaign.
Throughout the first half of 1951, the subcommittee heard
testimony from other witnesses. It investigated McCarthy's
role in the campaign, the apparently illegal amounts of
money spent by the Butler organization, publication of the
tabloid newspaper, use of the phony photograph, and the

[173]

strange midnight ride involving printer William Fedder. Senators McCarthy and Butler were invited to tell their sides of the story to the subcommittee, but declined.

On August 3, 1951, the subcommittee issued a unanimous report that severely criticized the activities of McCarthy, Butler, and others engaged in the campaign. Noting that the current rules of the Senate provided no basis for removing Butler from office, the panel recommended revising the rules to make it possible in the future to oust a senator if he used defamatory literature in a campaign. Moreover, in a direct slap at McCarthy, the subcommittee recommended the ouster of senators who acted improperly in campaigns in which they were not candidates.

Beyond the harm done to Tydings himself, the subcommittee described the broader damage done to society at large by irresponsible campaign tactics:

> If one candidate's campaign chooses to inject into an American election the poison of unfounded charges and doubts as to alleged subversive language, this tends to destroy not only the character of the candidate who is its target but also eats away like acid at the very fabric of American life. . . . It is not sufficient defense to say: "Let the people themselves judge the charges." The fact is that the people themselves are *not in possession of sufficient reliable information upon which to judge irresponsible accusations of disloyalty.* [Emphasis added.]

McCarthy characteristically issued a vitriolic response to the subcommittee report. Far from being humbled by the new condemnation of his conduct rendered by his Senate

[174]

colleagues, he became emboldened and sought ever more prominent targets for his charges of subversion. Perhaps his most daring attack came on June 14, 1951, when he took the Senate floor and delivered a 60,000-word speech denouncing the man considered by many the nation's most revered current hero—George C. Marshall.

After serving as army chief of staff during World War II and then as secretary of state, General Marshall had retired from government service in 1949. But when the United States had sent troops to help defend South Korea against an invasion by communist North Korean forces, President Truman had called Marshall back into the administration as secretary of defense. Marshall was a man of such dignity and solid reputation that it was unthinkable to many Americans that anyone would even question his loyalty. Yet, McCarthy did so in the strongest possible terms: "Unless we understand the record of Marshall, it will be impossible . . . to foretell the next move on the timetable of the great [communist] conspiracy."

He then went on to catalogue in great detail what he described as a long series of policies advocated by Marshall that supposedly played into the hands of the communists. Many dated back to World War II, when the Soviet Union had been an American ally. He blamed Marshall for the policy that had permitted communists to take control of mainland China and for other actions that he contended had strengthened communism's influence elsewhere in the world: "We have declined so precipitously in relation to the Soviet Union in the last six years, how much swifter may be our fall into disaster with Marshall at the [Defense Department] helm?"

Calling Marshall a member of a "crimson clique" with an "affinity for Chinese Reds," McCarthy continued:

[175]

"This must be the product of a great conspiracy, a conspiracy on a scale so immense as to dwarf any previous such venture in the history of man."

Marshall did not reply publicly to McCarthy's speech. But associates said he was sickened at the thought that a man of his reputation and long record of public service could be smeared by such an attack. Several months later, feeling that McCarthy's charges (though false) had diminished his usefulness, Marshall resigned as secretary of defense.

The attack on Marshall was one of many incidents that prompted Democratic Senator William Benton of Connecticut to introduce a resolution demanding that McCarthy resign or be subjected to an investigation to decide whether he should be expelled from the Senate. Experienced politicians, mindful of the fate that had befallen Millard Tydings and others who had opposed McCarthy, advised Benton against taking on the Wisconsin senator. But Benton, responding that he considered it a matter of conscience, refused to be deterred. In introducing the resolution seeking McCarthy's ouster, Benton called on him to refrain from taking part in Senate business until the matter could be resolved.

Benton pointed out that the full Senate had thus far taken no action on the report issued by Senator Gillette's subcommittee concerning the investigation of Butler and the Maryland election. But since he had no real expectation that McCarthy would resign, he asked the Senate Rules Committee to order the investigation. McCarthy replied with a statement that implied he would carry the battle to the people of Connecticut when Benton sought reelection.

Benton's call for a new investigation of McCarthy was

referred to Senator Gillette's subcommittee. On September 28, 1951, Benton appeared before the subcommittee and spelled out in detail the allegations he felt merited investigation. Among the charges he leveled were that McCarthy had lied to the Senate about his speech in Wheeling, West Virginia; that McCarthy had taken money contributed by citizens for his anticommunist crusade and converted it to his personal use; that his speech against General Marshall had consisted of "towering lies miles from honesty or honestly intended interpretation"; that he had repeatedly made false statements to the Senate; that he had played a leading role in what Benton called the "despicable" campaign against Senator Tydings; and that he had continually broken his promise never to make an accusation on the Senate floor that he would not repeat off the floor. Benton called McCarthy a man of "corruptibility and gross irresponsibility" who did not deserve to remain in the Senate.

Benton said a thorough investigation by the subcommittee should prove not only that McCarthy merited expulsion from the Senate, but also that McCarthy had committed criminal acts. He urged the subcommittee to send the results of its investigation to the Justice Department for possible criminal prosecution of McCarthy.

Senator Gillette invited McCarthy to appear before the subcommittee to reply to Benton's charges, but McCarthy declined in a letter to Gillette—filled with his usual vitriolic prose.

McCarthy also demanded that the two Republican members of the subcommittee, Senators Smith and Hendrickson, disqualify themselves from the investigation on the ground that they were prejudiced against him. As evidence of the alleged bias, he pointed out that they had signed both the "Declaration of Conscience" and the Gillette subcommittee report on the Maryland election. Both senators denied being prejudiced and declined to disqualify themselves.

Next, McCarthy leveled similar charges against a Democratic subcommittee member, Senator Hennings of Missouri. These charges were based on the fact that a law partner of Hennings, John R. Green, was serving as attorney for the editor of the *Daily Worker*, John Gates, in an appeal to the U.S. Supreme Court of a conspiracy conviction.

As an attorney, McCarthy obviously knew that legal ethics frequently required lawyers to represent clients whose views differed from their own. Yet, he tried to make it appear that there was something subversive about Green's representing Gates and Hennings's retaining Green as a partner.

Hennings, enraged by McCarthy's allegations, took the Senate floor and accused him of employing a "technique of distortion and misrepresentation." Hennings reminded the senators that Green's advocacy of the causes of unpopular clients had recently been praised by the *Journal of the American Bar Association* as representing "what is pure and noble in our profession."

The new investigation of McCarthy, conducted in fits and starts, stretched over almost a year and a half. The Gillette subcommittee sent investigators into various sections of the country to check on Benton's allegations. McCarthy, who was coming up for reelection in 1952, charged that the investigation was aimed at hurting his campaign.

In a letter to Gillette, McCarthy accused the subcommittee of dishonesty. He claimed that the investigators were working solely on "digging up campaign material against McCarthy." He added:

> . . . I cannot understand your being willing to label Guy Gillette as a man who will head a committee which is stealing from the pockets of the American taxpayers tens of thousands of dollars and then using this money to protect the Democratic Party from the political effect of the exposure of communists in government.

Members of the subcommittee, not surprisingly, became incensed at being called thieves. As for the "tens of thousands of dollars" McCarthy charged were being spent, the three-member subcommittee replied that total salaries and expenses devoted to the investigation totaled only $3,200.

Senator Monroney, as a test of confidence in the subcommittee, asked for a Senate vote on whether it should continue the McCarthy investigation or call it off. The vote was unanimous (with McCarthy absent) in favor of continuation.

While the investigation proceeded at a slow pace, political developments dominated the news. Not only was McCarthy up for reelection in 1952, but it was a presidential election year as well, and President Truman declined to run. The Democrats nominated Adlai E. Stevenson, governor of Illinois, as their presidential candidate.

At the Republican National Convention in Chicago, much to the dismay of many liberal members of the party, McCarthy was given an honored place as one of the main speakers. To the cheers of his avid supporters in the hall, McCarthy delivered a fighting speech: ". . . a rough fight is the only fight that communists understand. We can't fight communists in the . . . fashion of hitting them with a perfumed silk handkerchief at the front door while they batter our friends with brass knuckles at the back door." Referring to the war in Korea, McCarthy pledged that a Republican victory at the polls would ensure "we won't be in any war which we are afraid to win."

The convention chose as its presidential nominee General Dwight D. Eisenhower. Picked as the vice-presidential candidate was Richard Nixon, who had been elected to the Senate two years earlier largely on the basis of his work on the House Un-American Activities Committee.

Throughout his military career, Eisenhower had been extremely close to General George C. Marshall. Many wondered how he could support the reelection of McCarthy, who had accused Marshall of disloyalty to the country. Early in the campaign, when asked about McCarthy, Eisenhower indicated he might withhold his support: ". . . it is impossible for me to give what you might call blanket support to anyone . . . who holds views that would violate my conception of what is decent, right, just and fair."

Later, Eisenhower considered repudiating McCarthy by making a speech in Wisconsin defending General Marshall. Such a speech on McCarthy's home ground obviously would have represented a major embarrassment to him. Eisenhower went so far as to have his speech writer prepare an address, but McCarthy was told in advance of Eisenhower's plan. He and other Wisconsin Republicans met privately with the presidential candidate in Peoria, Illinois, and told him that such a speech would divide the party and hurt its chances in the campaign. The Wisconsin senator toured the state with Eisenhower, removing all doubt that he had the general's backing.

McCarthy made a series of speeches throughout the country in which he questioned the loyalty of Democratic presidential candidate Stevenson. In one speech, in Chicago, McCarthy charged that Stevenson—who had worked in the State Department and other federal agencies before being elected governor—was "part and parcel" of a conspiratorial group that included Alger Hiss and Owen Lattimore. Twice during the speech, McCarthy referred to Stevenson as "Alger—I mean Adlai." As threatened, McCarthy went into Connecticut and campaigned against Senator Benton.

On election day, Eisenhower and Nixon won the national race in a landslide. They carried into office with them enough Republican senators and congressmen to enable the party to take the control of both houses away from the Democrats. Eisenhower carried Wisconsin by more than 350,000 votes, and Republican Governor Walter Kohler by 407,000 votes. McCarthy was reelected, but his 139,000-vote margin was the lowest of any statewide candidate on the Wisconsin ballot. Still, he was assured of another six-year term in the Senate, and achieved further satisfaction from the fact that Connecticut voters defeated Senator Benton's reelection bid.

The subcommittee conducting the investigation of McCarthy waited until January 2, 1953—one day before the new Republican-controlled Congress was to take office—before issuing its report. It was sharply critical of McCarthy, particularly of his refusal to appear before the subcommittee. McCarthy's refusal to tell the subcommittee his side of the story "appears to reflect a disdain and contempt for the rules and wishes of the entire Senate." But knowing full well that the new Republican-controlled Senate would never agree to oust McCarthy, the subcommittee stopped short of urging the expulsion requested by Senator Benton. In fact, it made no recommendations at all. "The record should speak for itself," the report said. Once the new Senate entered office, the report was promptly buried; no further action was ever taken on it.

Republican control of both houses of Congress gave the party the chairmanship and majority membership on every congressional committee. Under the reorganization, McCarthy became chairman of the Senate Committee on Government Operations—which included a permanent subcommittee on investigations. McCarthy immediately announced that he would serve as chairman of the subcommittee as well as the parent body, and he lost no time in making clear that he intended to use this new source of power to continue pursuing the subject of alleged subversion in the government. Some observers had thought McCarthy might move on to other issues. After all, he had been claiming that a Republican administration would sweep the purported communists out of office in Washington.

As chief counsel to his committee, McCarthy hired a young New York lawyer named Roy M. Cohn who was to play a major role in future witch-hunt activities. Cohn, only twenty-five when he joined the committee staff, was considered a boy wonder of the legal profession. The son of a prominent New York State Supreme Court judge, he had received his degree from Columbia University Law School when just nineteen. After waiting two years to become old enough to take the bar examination, he became a federal prosecutor in New York and took part in the highly publicized trials of several alleged communists. Cohn was bright, tough, ambitious and, many said, ruthless—all qualities that appealed to McCarthy. Cohn, in turn, brought to the committee staff as "chief consultant" a twenty-five-year-old friend of his named G. David Schine, whose wealthy family owned the Schine hotel chain. Together, Cohn and Schine would become two of the most controversial staff members in the history of congressional committees.

McCarthy's first investigation as committee chairman concerned the "Voice of America," a radio program through which the State Department broadcasts propaganda and other material to listeners in foreign countries. Before beginning hearings on the matter, McCarthy leaked to newsmen numerous stories claiming he had uncovered widespread subversion among "Voice" staff members. But the "evidence" produced later at the hearings amounted to little more than speculation and gossip.

The main focus of the hearings was the construction by the "Voice" of two huge radio transmitters. In an attempt to prevent the broadcasts from reaching listeners in communist-controlled countries, the Soviet Union was resorting to a technique known as jamming—in which electronic interference was beamed into the atmosphere to block out the American programs. The "Voice" built the two most powerful short-wave transmitters in the world with the hope that they would counter the jamming. One transmitter, known as Baker East, was placed near Wilmington, North Carolina. The other, Baker West, was built near Seattle, Washington.

McCarthy charged that the sites chosen were the worst possible in the country because atmospheric conditions there caused interference that disrupted radio signals. And he claimed that deliberate sabotage, carried out by subversive "Voice" officials, had been responsible for selection of the sites.

[183]

Actually, the State Department—knowing that atmospheric interference could be a critical problem—had taken great pains to choose the best possible locations for the transmitters. It had assembled an advisory panel of experts from such organizations as the Massachusetts Institute of Technology's Research Laboratory of Electronics, the U.S. Army Signal Corps, the U.S. Bureau of Standards, and the Radio Corporation of America's Radio Propagation Laboratory to help make the decision. On the basis of this panel's recommendations, the sites near Wilmington and Seattle were chosen.

But one engineer employed by the "Voice," Lewis McKesson, differed with the panel's findings. McKesson was so adamant in his views that "Voice" officials asked the research laboratory at MIT to make a new evaluation of the situation. After doing so, experts at the laboratory firmly supported the original decision. The laboratory's director, Dr. Jerome B. Wiesner (later to serve as science adviser to Presidents John F. Kennedy and Lyndon B. Johnson), wrote to "Voice" officials that the methods used by McKesson in examining the problem were "so oversimplified as to lead to erroneous conclusions."

Yet, McCarthy made the disgruntled McKesson the star witness at his hearings. Ignoring the opinions of the experts who chose the transmitter sites—in fact, refusing to hear testimony from them—McCarthy simply took McKesson's word for it that the worst possible locations had been selected. He then asked McKesson a series of loaded questions designed to put into the hearing record the implication that sabotage, committed by subversives, had resulted in selection of poor locations.

"Voice of America" officials, unnerved by McCarthy's investigation, which was greatly aided by Roy Cohn, asked

[184]

the MIT laboratory to make one more study of the transmitter locations to be absolutely certain the previous decisions had been wise. The new study upheld the original choices.

McCarthy, unable to prove his sabotage allegation, wound up the investigation of the transmitter locations by issuing a report claiming that the hearings "suggest deliberate sabotage as a possible alternative to hopeless incompetence." The State Department, reacting to the aura of suspicion and fearing the risks of further antagonizing McCarthy, decided to abandon the projects. The transmitters, which had cost more than $8,000,000, were dismantled and placed in storage. No "communist" sabotage plot could have been more successful—yet McCarthy expressed satisfaction with the outcome: he had won what he considered a victory over the State Department.

The disastrous consequences that can result from political witch hunts were demonstrated a short time after the hearings on the transmitters. A great deal of the planning for the transmitters had been done by a "Voice of America" engineer named Raymond Kaplan. McCarthy's allegations of sabotage, Kaplan felt, unfairly cast doubt on his personal loyalty. Amid the continuing suspicion, Kaplan committed suicide by jumping in front of a truck in Boston. McCarthy, denying that he was in any way to blame for the suicide, said he had uncovered no evidence of wrongdoing by Kaplan. But Kaplan, in a note to his family, said he was taking his life because of the McCarthy hearings. He said that he had been made "the patsy" in McCarthy's investigation: "You see, once the dogs are set upon you, everything you have done from the beginning of time is suspect."

After the close of the hearings on the "Voice of Amer-

[185]

ica," McCarthy turned his attention to its parent organization in the State Department—the International Information Administration (IIA). In addition to directing the "Voice" operations, the IIA maintained libraries in foreign countries, produced films, published various materials, and conducted other activities to further the government's interests abroad. McCarthy launched a new witch hunt, charging that some of the IIA officials were "doing a rather effective job of sabotaging . . . Eisenhower's foreign policy."

As one of his main targets, McCarthy chose Reed Harris, deputy director of the IIA, who had a distinguished record in public service. McCarthy discovered that, twenty-one years earlier, Harris had been suspended from Columbia University: he had written a book criticizing the undue emphasis on athletics in colleges, and had written editorials in the Columbia student newspaper regarded by campus administrators as being in poor taste. Obviously a man with that background did not belong in an important position in the IIA. Worse, McCarthy discovered, Harris had been offered help by the American Civil Liberties Union (ACLU) in fighting his suspension from the university.

Neither the U.S. Justice Department, the FBI, nor any congressional committee had ever listed the ACLU as a communist front—yet McCarthy drew subversive inferences from Harris's representation by an ACLU lawyer. After persistent harassment by McCarthy, Harris finally resigned in disgust.

Following this triumph, McCarthy sent Cohn and Schine on a European tour to investigate IIA activities. The young men hopscotched through twelve cities in seventeen days, at the taxpayers' cost of more than $8,000, and became the laughing stock of the European press. The "Rover

Boys" (as they were called in Vienna) did make one great find in the IIA-maintained library in Vienna: an obviously subversive American writer—because his work was also circulated by the Soviet library in Vienna—Mark Twain.

While these capers were going on, Eisenhower appointed Dr. Robert L. Johnson, president of Temple University, as the IIA administrator. Johnson then named Martin Merson as his chief aide. The two men soon found themselves inundated by demands from McCarthy to drastically cut the agency's budget and staff, to fire certain employees, and to hire others. Eventually the IIA's 9,000 employees were investigated; six were regarded as security risks (though not necessarily subversive), and were fired. McCarthy was not satisfied, and Merson and Johnson were subjected to further harassment and demands by Cohn and Schine. The fear of McCarthy had become so great that many officials of the executive branch were beginning to knuckle under—including Johnson and Merson. Under pressure, Johnson ordered the discharge of 1,500 employees. McCarthy was irate: unwittingly, Johnson had fired some of McCarthy's network of secret informers in the agency.

McCarthy continued to hound the IIA. His next step was a new series of hearings involving the authors of various books circulated by the IIA libraries abroad. The authors were private citizens, not public officials; they had not asked that their books be included in the IIA library collections. Yet, by virtue of the mere fact that their works appeared on the IIA library shelves, they were obliged to appear at the televised hearings and defend their writings, their political beliefs, and their associations with other persons.

Many of McCarthy's critics charged that he was violat-

WITCH HUNT

ing the freedom of expression guaranteed by the First
Amendment in calling upon the authors to answer for
their writings. This issue was emphasized when McCarthy
called as a witness the editor of the *New York Post*, James
Wechsler. In April 1934, while a college student, Wechsler
had become a member of the Young Communist League
(YCL)—a fact he never tried to conceal. But he had quit
the organization in 1937, at the age of twenty-two, and
had become a vigorous anticommunist. His newspaper,
while opposing communism, had also been among the
nation's foremost critics of McCarthy, members of HUAC,
and other witch hunters. McCarthy claimed that several
books written by Wechsler—which he was never able to
identify—had been found on the shelves of IIA libraries.
It was on that supposed basis that he called Wechsler as
a witness on April 24, 1953. But the questioning revealed
that McCarthy was far more interested in Wechsler's role
as editor of a newspaper critical of witch hunters than
he was in Wechsler's authorship of the books.

After Roy Cohn had led Wechsler through a discussion
of his career—including his brief membership in the YCL
—McCarthy took over the questioning in his tireless
manner, and with considerable sparring with Wechsler. He
began by asking if there were people working for him on
the newspaper who were or had been members of the
YCL—a question that obviously had nothing to do with
the ostensible subject of the hearings, the IIA libraries.
Wechsler replied that McCarthy was broaching a topic
"which the American Society of Newspaper Editors might
want to consider at length." He then added: "To my
knowledge, there are no communists on the staff of the
New York Post at this time."

McCarthy was not satisfied, and asked if there were

any former communists on the newspaper's staff. Wechsler replied that there were four—whom he named—all of whom he said had left the Communist Party years earlier and become staunch anticommunists. McCarthy appeared unconvinced, and told him:

> You see, your books—some of them—were paid for by taxpayers' money. They are being used, allegedly, to fight communism. Your record, as far as I can see it, has not been to fight communism. You have fought every man who has ever tried to fight communism, as far as I know. Your paper, in my opinion, is next to and almost paralleling the *Daily Worker*. We are curious to know, therefore, why your books were purchased.

Wechsler replied that, contrary to McCarthy's statements, his record of anticommunism was well known. He pointed out that he had frequently been the target of severe criticism by the Communist Party and the *Daily Worker*. As an example, he read into the hearing record a resolution denouncing him that had been adopted by the Communist Party Central Committee on December 28, 1952. "I am rather fond of this tribute," Wechsler said, referring to the resolution. "And it may perhaps have some bearing on your comment that I have not been active in fighting communism."

In reply to this, McCarthy asked if Wechsler or anyone on his staff had taken part in promoting the party resolution. Wechsler was so astonished at the suggestion that he could or would promote a resolution denouncing himself that he responded: "Is that a serious question?"

After this contentious exchange was settled, McCarthy

turned to questioning Wechsler about the editorial policies of the *Post* and whether he had always been critical of the heads of the House Un-American Activities Committee.

Wechsler replied that he could not recall ever writing editorials in support of J. Parnell Thomas, the former HUAC chairman who had wound up in jail. But he read into the record a 1950 letter from Richard Nixon, then a member of the committee, praising a *Post* editorial on the Alger Hiss case as "one of the most able and fair appraisals of a very difficult problem which I have seen."

MCCARTHY: The principal villains in your book are those who have gone about exposing communists. Is that correct? Or is that an unfair statement?

WECHSLER: No, Senator, that is not correct. I may say . . . that we have repeatedly taken the position that the *New York Post* is as bitterly opposed to Joe Stalin as it is to Joe McCarthy, and we believe that a free society can combat both.

McCarthy continued to insinuate that Wechsler might not really have severed his connections with communism —that his formal resignation from the YCL sixteen years earlier might have been a mere sham. He asked Wechsler to submit a list of all league members he had known. Wechsler replied that he was not sure he could remember all of them.

Wechsler cited editorial after editorial that he had written for the *Post* opposing the aims of communism. He said he would be glad to submit for the hearing record copies of every editorial published by the *Post* during his editorship. "I do not think that I would care to read them," McCarthy replied. "I read enough of your stuff, Mr. Wechsler, to find that your paper, so far as I know, always leads the vanguard, with the *Daily Worker*. . . ."

After permitting Wechsler to enter in the record various exhibits indicating his opposition to communism, McCarthy asked him that, if he were a communist and wished to advance that cause, would it not be "the most effective way" to claim he had left the party, gain control of a newspaper, and use it against those who were actually fighting communism.

Wechsler answered that he doubted the communists used such tactics. He pointed out that McCarthy's committee had a former communist, Howard Rushmore, on the staff, but that did not mean the communists had infiltrated the committee. McCarthy responded that Rushmore was a different kind of former communist from Wechsler, since he had often volunteered to testify before congressional committees about his former associates.

Wechsler replied: "Senator, let's face it. You are saying that an ex-communist who is for McCarthy is a good one and an ex-communist who is against McCarthy is a suspect. I will stand on that distinction." McCarthy said that was not so—that the real test of an ex-communist's sincerity was how many of his former associates he agreed to expose. It was the old story of the witch hunter's passion for names, names, and more names.

The discussion between McCarthy and Wechsler continued on the question of whether Wechsler felt he was being treated unfairly by the committee, whether he felt he had been intimidated or abused. Wechsler replied that he questioned the very nature of the proceedings and regarded them as an attempt to intimidate both himself

[191]

and other editors, smear the *New York Post,* and invade newspapers' rights to speak independently and in opposition to the McCarthy committee.

The hearing was adjourned with the expectation that Wechsler would be recalled if he decided to comply with McCarthy's demand to provide a list of his former colleagues in the YCL. As Wechsler subsequently explained in a book he wrote dealing with his confrontation with McCarthy, *The Age of Suspicion,* he was torn by conflicting thoughts about preparing such a list:

> I did not see how I could persuade my perplexed countrymen that unwillingness to entrust such a list to McCarthy was different from the now stereotyped refusal of communists to answer questions before congressional committees. . . . Having decided that silence was exactly what he was inviting, I had chosen to talk; I could not balk now. My concern, of course, was not for anyone on the list who had remained a communist; it was for those who might have renounced communism as I had, but who might occupy positions where they were more vulnerable to attack. . . .

Wechsler decided to provide the list, but to try to prevent McCarthy from making it public in order to protect the rights of those named. On May 5, 1953, he was called back before the McCarthy committee. After preliminary discussion, Wechsler was permitted to read a prepared statement.

Wechsler's detailed statement reiterated much of what he had said in the hearing, but even further emphasized his belief that "the paramount issue is the attack which

[192]

Senator McCarthy is waging upon freedom of the press."

He reminded the committee that most individuals who joined the YCL did so out of youthful idealism during a period of national insecurity and uncertainty following the Depression, and at a time when "the rise of aggressive fascism . . . blinded many of them to the basic similarities between communism and fascism." He said that the majority of those on his list were not "professional, hardened communists" but were primarily engaged in demonstrations for peace, academic freedom, and union organizing. He noted that the committee considered his earlier statements "unsatisfactory" because they were "insufficiently dramatic": "Unlike some other former communists who have appeared before congressional committees, my experience was comparatively brief and distinctly unhistoric. I never got any 'pumpkin papers.' "

Wechsler concluded his statement with another assertion that McCarthy's inquiry into his past activities was "designed to silence independent newspaper comment." He then made a final plea for the former YCL colleagues: ". . . I ask the committee to insure protection for those on the list who may be the innocent victims of this proceeding."

Eventually, the committee did agree to refrain from making the list public. But that was small consolation to Wechsler, who saw the freedom-of-the-press issue as the basic consideration. As promised, he requested an investigation by the American Society of Newspaper Editors of what he regarded as McCarthy's attempt to limit press freedom.

Basil Walters, the society's chairman, appointed a committee of eleven newspaper editors to study the transcript of McCarthy's hearings involving Wechsler. After reviewing the matter, the committee was unable to reach unanimous agreement on whether McCarthy's conduct constituted violation of freedom of the press. While none of the eleven defended McCarthy's actions, the committee said its members were divided on whether "this single interchange constituted a clear and present danger to freedom of the press justifying a specific challenge."

Wechsler, throughout his dispute with McCarthy, received strong support from his employer, *Post* publisher Dorothy Schiff. But some other authors whose books were discovered in IIA libraries were not so fortunate. These were not persons who made their livings primarily by writing books; they held full-time jobs and did their writing outside working hours. They were bluntly told by their employers that they would be fired unless they were "cleared" by McCarthy. And the usual way to get "cleared" was to tell McCarthy exactly what he wanted to hear— they provided McCarthy with long lists of names of former associates and assured him they thought he was performing valuable service in conducting the hearings. Then, with his blessing, they were permitted to retain their jobs.

McCarthy presented IIA officials with a new list of 418 authors, demanding to know how their books had come to be circulated in the overseas libraries. Among the 418 persons were some of the most prominent names in American literature—many of them authors whose anticommunist views were well known. Those listed included Sherwood Anderson, Theodore Dreiser, Stephen Vincent Benét, Archibald MacLeish, Edmund Wilson, W. H. Auden, Edna Ferber, and Arthur Schlesinger, Jr.

Although McCarthy's questioning of the loyalty of many such writers seemed baseless, the State Department again decided to back away from a confrontation with him. It ordered IIA officials to remove from the library shelves books by authors found offensive to the Wisconsin senator. In a few cases, IIA personnel went so far as to burn the books in question. That step, which echoed the book-burning era of the Nazis, was too much for Secretary of State John Foster Dulles. He ruled out any future burning of books.

President Eisenhower, who had remained aloof from the controversy, finally became involved in an indirect way on June 14, 1953. He used the occasion of. a graduation speech at Dartmouth College to speak out against suppression of ideas:

> Don't join the book-burners. Don't think you are going to conceal thoughts by concealing the evidence that they ever existed. Don't be afraid to go to the library and read every book so long as it does not offend your own ideas of decency. That should be the only censorship.

Although Eisenhower later told a press conference that his remarks were not intended as criticism of any individual since he did not want to deal in personalities, the speech was generally regarded as a rebuke to McCarthy.

The following month, there was another indication of a stiffening of administration policy in relation to McCarthy. The State Department disclosed a new order concerning books in IIA libraries. Books would no longer be banned from the libraries solely because of the identities and political ideologies of their authors. They would be banned only if their specific contents—after study by government officials—were regarded as injurious to the national interest. Of course, a measure of censorship would still be involved, but it would at least be carried out on a more rational basis than in the immediate past.

A short time later, McCarthy dropped his investigation of the IIA and moved on to other subjects. But his harassment of IIA officials had taken a heavy toll. The agency's ranks had been sharply cut, its efficiency had been curtailed, and its morale had reached low ebb. After only five months on the job, during which he had spent much of his time fending off attacks by McCarthy, Dr. Robert Johnson resigned as IIA administrator.

The IIA was subsequently reorganized and given a new name—the United States Information Agency. But no matter what its organizational structure or name, the agency would take years to recover from the ravages of the McCarthy era.

SOURCES AND SUPPLEMENTARY READING

Richard H. Rovere's *Senator Joe McCarthy*, Fred J. Cook's *The Nightmare Decade*, and Lately Thomas's *When Even Angels Wept* were valuable sources of information for this chapter.

Newspaper and magazine articles, supplemented by transcripts of Senate committee hearings, provided additional material.

The most comprehensive discussion of *New York Post* editor James Wechsler's conflicts with McCarthy is contained in Wechsler's book, *The Age of Suspicion* (Random House, 1953). The book also includes a candid account of Wechsler's youthful flirtation with communism and describes the manner in which it came back to haunt him in later life. The less than honest treatment Wechsler received at the hands of some of his journalistic colleagues —particularly those who ardently supported McCarthy— provides an interesting case history of the witch-hunt mentality at work in the news media.

11

★ ★ ★

McCarthy versus the Army

Senator Joseph McCarthy, it seemed, was at the height of his power in mid-1953. Despite periodic setbacks, he had become a figure whose very name struck fear into the hearts of countless officials in both the executive and legislative branches of government—not to mention private citizens. There was no way of predicting where he would strike next or how far he would go in extending his influence. On the surface, at least, all indications were that his political strength would continue to grow.

But although nobody knew it at the time, events were contriving to deal serious blows to McCarthy's career. These events began with McCarthy's decision to hire J. B. Matthews, the controversial former investigator for HUAC, as executive director of his investigating committee. On June 22, 1953, without consulting any other members of the committee, McCarthy announced the appointment of Matthews. Since leaving the committee,

Matthews had served as a "consultant" on communism to various public and private groups and had written on the subject for the Hearst newspaper chain and several right-wing magazines.

He had barely taken over his duties with the McCarthy committee when he suddenly became the center of a storm of controversy. The furor concerned an article, "Reds and Our Churches," that Matthews had written for the July issue of the *American Mercury* magazine. The article began: "The largest single group supporting the communist apparatus in the United States today is composed of Protestant clergymen." It went on to charge that in the previous seventeen years the Communist Party had enlisted the support of a least 7,000 clergymen as "party members, fellow travelers, espionage agents, party-line adherents and unwitting dupes." Matthews had arrived at the 7,000 figure by adding up the names of clergymen he found on petitions, advertisements, and the like supporting all manner of causes that were also backed by the communists. His article did not contain any information corroborating his espionage charge; nor did it name even a single clergyman alleged to be a card-carrying communist.

Throughout the country, clergymen and laymen alike thundered their outrage at the article, at Matthews, and at McCarthy. Within his own committee, among those who formerly supported McCarthy as well as those critical of him, many joined in the general protest, denounced Matthews, and demanded that McCarthy fire him.

McCarthy tried to shrug off the uproar, arguing that Matthews had written the article before he was hired, and also had written it with the best of intentions. He said to newsmen: "As a free-lance writer, [Matthews] wrote many articles. I have not read them and don't intend to. I do not set myself up as a censor."

McCarthy seriously misjudged the depth of resentment touched off by the Matthews affair. Clergymen across the country took to their pulpits to assail his charges. Senators and other Washington officials were inundated by complaints. At a special meeting of the McCarthy committee, the vote to fire Matthews was 4 to 3, but McCarthy refused to abide by the decision, saying that, as chairman, he alone had the right to determine who would serve on the committee staff.

Officials at the White House had been increasingly disturbed by McCarthy's tactics, and had been awaiting an opportunity to cut him down to size. They saw in the Matthews affair a chance for President Eisenhower to speak out strongly against McCarthy—but were aware he would need some excuse to make a public statement without appearing to intrude in a congressional dispute.

Accordingly, presidential speech writer Emmet John Hughes and the president's chief of staff, Sherman Adams, arranged for officials of the National Conference of Christians and Jews to send Eisenhower a telegram protesting the Matthews article—which they were only too glad to compose. The telegram was released to the press; meanwhile, presidential aides had prepared a reply for Eisenhower to issue: the total effect was a sharp rebuke to both Matthews and McCarthy. Realizing that he could no longer stand up to such pressure of public opinion and political power, McCarthy reluctantly announced that he accepted Matthew's resignation. It was one of the first times McCarthy had been forced to back down from a strongly held position. More important, it was the first open break between McCarthy and his fellow Republican in the White House.

In an attempt to divert attention from the embarrassing defeat he had suffered, McCarthy immediately launched a new attack. His target was the Central Intelligence Agency (CIA), the nation's chief spy and counterspy organization. In a Senate speech on July 10, 1953, McCarthy accused CIA official William P. Bundy (who happened to be the son-in-law of former Secretary of State Dean Acheson) of contributing $400 to a fund used to pay the legal expenses of Alger Hiss during his long court battles.

Of course, Bundy had every right to contribute the money. He might have believed Hiss was innocent or, even if he had no idea of Hiss's guilt or innocence, he might have felt the American system of justice entitled him to an adequate defense. But McCarthy insisted on placing a sinister interpretation on the contribution, and questioned whether anyone who had donated to the defense fund was fit to serve in the CIA.

In his Senate speech, McCarthy said that he wanted to question Bundy but the CIA official had "suddenly disappeared" when he found out about this intention. Later, a CIA official reported that he had talked to Bundy and had been told that CIA policy barred any employee of the agency from appearing before the McCarthy committee. McCarthy claimed to be outraged and said he intended to subpoena CIA Director Allen Dulles—the brother of Secretary of State John Foster Dulles—to testify before the committee.

Actually, the CIA policy on congressional testimony was well known. The agency's work was so secret that its officials were permitted to testify before only a few specified congressional committees—and McCarthy's committee was not one of them. Members of the Senate and House who did not serve on the specified committees were not even aware of the amount of the CIA budget.

Democratic Senator Mike Monroney of Oklahoma took the Senate floor to denounce McCarthy's threat to investigate the CIA—arguing that such an investigation would reveal "to our enemies information . . . that even the Kremlin's best spy apparatus could not get for them." Ridiculing McCarthy and his aides as "Keystone Cops," Monroney said:

> I question the oft-stated claim that only the senator from Wisconsin stands between us and complete internal subversion. I doubt that he has a monopoly within this government of despising, exposing and prosecuting communists and their fellow travelers. I doubt that Messrs. Cohn and Schine . . . or even the distinguished junior senator from Wisconsin measure up in ability to the Federal Bureau of Investigation.

In view of the investigation of the CIA in the mid-1970s, McCarthy's attack against the agency seems little more than an ironic flurry. Shortly after Senator Monroney's speech to the Senate, McCarthy met privately with CIA Director Dulles, and then announced that he was abandoning his plan to investigate the agency: the threat to conduct the investigation had served its purpose by drawing attention away from the J. B. Matthews affair.

But other embarrassments awaited him. The Democratic members of his committee—Senators McClellan, Jackson,

[202]

and Symington—renewed their demand for a greater voice in its operations. Having helped bring about the ouster of Matthews, they now insisted on being given partial control over the selection and direction of the committee staff. The three Democrats forced the issue to a committee vote, but this time all four Republican members voted against them. Although McCarthy's position had been upheld, the victory was a hollow one.

McClellan, Jackson, and Symington abruptly resigned from the committee, charging that McCarthy's sole control over the staff put them in an "impossible situation—having responsibility but no voice, right or authority." All other Democratic members of the Senate supported the resignations, refusing to fill the vacant seats on the committee. McCarthy tried to play down the importance of the resignations, saying: "It's the old Democratic policy of either rule or ruin."

But there was no way of disguising the fact that McCarthy had suffered another reverse. When a committee chairman's policies became so outrageous that he could not persuade a single member of the opposition party to serve with him, the obvious conclusion was that something was radically wrong with the chairman or his policies. And even more than in the past, future actions by the committee were bound to be tainted by intimations of partisan politics.

McCarthy had no way of knowing it at the time, but events would bring him still greater problems—major ones that would dwarf those he had previously confronted. These events began in the summer of 1953 when it became known that the government, in the ordinary course of business, planned to draft G. David Schine into the army. McCarthy and Roy Cohn decided that

[203]

it would never do for Schine to be treated as just another draftee, a lowly private. McCarthy summoned Major General Miles Reber, head of the army's branch in charge of dealing with members of Congress. He told Reber that he wanted Schine to be given permission to enlist in the army with the rank of lieutenant. Reber said he would discuss the request with other officials and see what could be done. Several of the army's highest officers—well aware that McCarthy might severely harass them if he did not get his way—were involved in the discussions. In the end, they decided that Schine should not be given any special consideration and the commission should be denied.

After Schine was notified of the decision, Cohn inquired of the navy and air force whether they would be willing to give Schine a direct commission as an officer. They also declined. McCarthy and Schine decided that, if they could not get Schine a higher rank than private in the army, they would at least try to see to it that he received special privileges once inducted. On October 2, Cohn and Francis Carr, a former FBI agent who had replaced J. B. Matthews as executive director of the McCarthy committee, appeared for a meeting at the office of no lesser official than Secretary of the Army Robert T. Stevens.

They told Stevens they had two important items to discuss. The first was that McCarthy planned to launch an investigation into alleged subversion at the U.S. Army Signal Corps laboratory at Fort Monmouth, New Jersey. The second was the question of what could be done to make army life pleasant for G. David Schine. Cohn said he considered it essential that, once Schine entered the army, he be stationed somewhere in the New York–New Jersey area—so he would be available for consultation on the Fort Monmouth investigation. The implication created by the combined discussion on Fort Monmouth and Schine was that McCarthy might give the army a particularly rough going-over in his investigation if Schine were not accorded special treatment. Secretary Stevens said he felt Schine should receive the same treatment as any other recruit. The meeting ended without any agreement.

In succeeding weeks, Cohn telephoned or visited Stevens and other army officials almost every day to renew his demands for Schine. At one point he was told that the army did not feel it would be in the national interest to give Schine privileges denied the other 300,000 men inducted annually. A report later issued by the army on the Schine affair said: "Mr. Cohn replied that, if the national interest was what the Army wanted, he'd give it a little and then proceeded to outline how he would expose the Army in its worst light and show the country how shabbily it is being run."

In the end, the army did agree to make some concessions. Schine was formally inducted on November 3, 1953, but given a week's grace before reporting for duty. His assigned base was Fort Dix, New Jersey. The day after his arrival, Roy Cohn and Francis Carr showed up and impressed upon the base commander, Major General Cornelius Ryan, that Schine was an important man who would need considerable time off from his army duties to help the McCarthy committee. Although army recruits were rarely allowed visitors immediately after reporting for duty, Cohn and Carr were permitted to visit Schine. Likewise, against normal army regulations, Schine was given a weekend pass just two days after his arrival.

Other special treatment followed. Schine received passes to leave the base almost every night—often returning in

[205]

the small hours of the morning. He was excused from Kitchen Police assignments, guard duty, and rifle practice. He addressed his superior officers by their first names, rather than their ranks, and otherwise made it clear that he had no intention of being treated as just another recruit.

All of this became too much for the base commander, General Ryan. He telephoned the U.S. Army Chief Attorney John G. Adams and said that, unless ordered otherwise, he planned at least to stop giving Schine passes on week nights. Even this slight denial of privileges brought immediate complaints from Roy Cohn. Innumerable contretemps followed, with Cohn, Carr, and McCarthy pitted against high government and army officials. The less satisfied McCarthy and his aides were with the treatment accorded to Schine, the more severely the McCarthy committee harassed the army over Fort Monmouth—and McCarthy was dominating the front pages with charges that the Army Signal Corps laboratory there had been infiltrated by communist spies.

If true, McCarthy's charges would have been serious indeed. For the Signal Corps laboratory at the fort was working on projects that involved some of the nation's most sensitive military secrets. The projects included the latest types of radar devices and other electronic systems designed to detect or deter attacks by potential enemies.

There had been a previous investigation of suspected subversion at Fort Monmouth. In late 1951, a Signal Corps intelligence officer called for a congressional investigation of what he contended were lax security measures at Fort Monmouth. He claimed that fifty-seven secret documents were missing from the laboratory files.

The investigation disclosed that these documents were not missing at all.

Nevertheless, McCarthy decided to stage his own investigation. He conducted a series of secret hearings at the federal courthouse in New York. Each day, McCarthy would emerge from the hearing room and brief newsmen on what had been going on behind the closed doors. Since he was the only person giving out any information, the reporters took his word for it that the accounts were accurate.

By the time the flimsiness of his claims about Fort Monmouth became apparent, McCarthy had long since moved on to other investigations and allegations. He continued checking on various army operations, and eventually came up with a case that was destined to receive attention out of all proportion to its actual importance. The case involved Dr. Irving Peress, an army dentist.

Shortly after the United States entered the Korean War, it became apparent that there was a critical shortage of medical personnel. To fill the need, the government ordered a special draft requiring all doctors and dentists to register with their draft boards. Peress registered, and applied for an army commission. (It was standard procedure for military doctors and dentists to be commissioned as officers.)

Peress entered the army on October 15, 1952, and was assigned to the Dental Corps. Two weeks later, he was routinely asked to fill out a loyalty questionnaire. In response to three questions on the form, Peress pleaded the Fifth Amendment. The questions asked whether he was or ever had been a "member of any organization which advocates the overthrow of our constitutional government by unconstitutional means."

Army officers, bogged down with paperwork, apparently did not spot these answers for several months.

During February 1953, intelligence officers at First Army Headquarters in New York checked Peress's loyalty questionnaire. They discovered he had pleaded the Fifth Amendment, and ordered an investigation. First Army officials, after reviewing the results of the investigation, recommended to the Pentagon that Peress be discharged as a security risk. Months dragged by, with other officers supporting the recommendation for Peress's discharge, but without final action being taken.

In the meantime, Congress amended the draft law to provide that doctors and dentists called into military service should be promoted to ranks "commensurate with . . . [their] professional education, experience and ability." Peress, then stationed at Camp Kilmer, New Jersey, applied for a promotion to major. On October 21, 1953, the commanding officer at Camp Kilmer, Brigadier General Ralph Zwicker, recommended to First Army Headquarters that Peress be immediately discharged. Two days later, despite that recommendation, Peress received his promotion to major. (It should be noted that he was one of about 7,000 army doctors and dentists receiving promotions around the same time.)

During December 1953, army personnel officials in Washington decided it was imperative to get Peress out of the service. The question was how to do it. There did not seem to be any grounds for a court-martial—Peress had apparently not violated any army regulations; his dental work while in the service had been satisfactory; he had not disobeyed orders. Similarly, there seemed no grounds for giving Peress a dishonorable discharge. All that remained was an honorable discharge. On January 18, 1954, the Pentagon ordered that Peress be given an honorable discharge—permitting him to choose any date within the next ninety days for his separation from the service. He initially chose March 31.

Meanwhile, Senator McCarthy got wind of the matter, decided to investigate, and summoned Peress to testify at a hearing in New York on January 30. McCarthy asked Peress if anyone in the army had ever asked him if he was a member of the Communist Party. Peress declined to answer, pleading the Fifth Amendment to twenty-three other questions asked at the hearing—all concerning his possible communist activities or connections.

It is interesting to note that McCarthy jumped to the conclusion that Peress was a communist because he had pleaded the Fifth. McCarthy then remarked that apparently Peress was to be given an honorable discharge, and asked him why he had been requested to resign. Peress replied: "They wouldn't tell me the reason." The hearing was adjourned, but McCarthy told Peress he would be called back at a later date for further questioning.

Two days later, McCarthy sent a letter to Army Secretary Stevens—insisting that Peress not be given an honorable discharge. He also demanded that the army court-martial "those responsible officers who had full knowledge of [Peress's] communist activities and either took no steps to have him removed or were responsible for his promotion thereafter." Stevens was out of the country on official business when McCarthy's letter arrived.

Although Peress knew nothing about the letter, he visited his commanding officer, General Zwicker, on the day after it was sent and asked that his discharge take effect immediately. Since Zwicker had previously been ordered to allow Peress to choose any discharge date within the next ninety days, he granted the request. Peress left the army the same day with an honorable discharge. When he learned of the discharge, McCarthy became irate and renewed his demand for the court-martial of any officer involved in promoting Peress or granting him an honorable discharge.

On February 18, McCarthy resumed hearings in New York. When Peress was called to the witness chair, he began his testimony by reading a prepared statement. "I have been subpoenaed . . . to answer certain questions concerning my political beliefs. . . . So that there may be no mistake about my position in this regard, I shall decline to answer any such questions under the protection of the Fifth Amendment to the Constitution." Peress continued to plead the Fifth Amendment to a succession of questions, and McCarthy waved him away from the witness chair and summoned General Zwicker to testify.

Zwicker, a West Point graduate, had been a World War II hero—winning such decorations as the Silver Star, the Legion of Merit with oak-leaf cluster, the Bronze Star with two clusters, and the French Legion of Honor and Croix de Guerre with palm. On D-Day, he had led a special reconnaissance squad ashore at Normandy, France. Later, he had commanded an infantry regiment that had made a vital stand in the Battle of the Bulge.

In the Peress case, Zwicker had merely followed the orders of his superiors. But McCarthy, ignoring Zwicker's distinguished record and his subordinate role in the affair, treated the general as if he were the defendant in a trial. He tried to make Zwicker responsible for explaining the decisions to give Peress the promotion and honorable discharge. Zwicker, for his part, played into McCarthy's hands by providing several evasive and contradictory answers.

McCarthy insisted on an explanation of why Zwicker had not delayed Peress's discharge, pending further investigation of his loyalty. Zwicker said he had no authority, under the orders from his superiors, to delay the discharge.

McCarthy posed a hypothetical question: Suppose an officer under Zwicker's command had just been accused of stealing fifty dollars. Would he allow the man to be discharged before the reported theft was investigated? Zwicker said he would have the matter investigated before letting the man out of army jurisdiction.

The assumption of McCarthy's question, however, was misleading. A base commander, such as Zwicker, had the authority to supervise the investigation of a minor theft. In security matters, he was obliged to leave the investigation to intelligence officers assigned by higher headquarters. But McCarthy refused to accept the distinction.

Zwicker stated that all the information about Peress made public in the McCarthy hearings was known to the army officials who ordered the discharge "long prior to the time that you ever called this man for investigation."

This exchange created further difficulties for Zwicker. McCarthy asked other hypothetical questions: Should a general who had acted as Zwicker had in the Peress case "be removed from the military"? Zwicker replied: "He should by all means be kept [in the military] if he were acting under competent orders to separate [discharge] that man." Should the general who initiated the order to give the honorable discharge be kept in the army? Zwicker said such a decision would not be his to make.

MCCARTHY: You are ordered to answer. You are an employee of the people. I want to know how you feel about getting rid of communists.

ZWICKER: I do not think he should be removed from the military.

MCCARTHY: Then, General, you should be removed from any command. Any man who has been given the honor of being promoted to general and who says, "I will protect another general who protected communists," is not fit to wear that uniform, General. [Zwicker, of course, had made no such statement.] I think it is a tremendous disgrace to have this sort of thing given to the public.

When Army Secretary Stevens learned of the treatment Zwicker had been given before the committee, he became enraged at McCarthy. On February 21, Stevens issued an order forbidding Zwicker and all other army officers to testify before the McCarthy committee. In a telephone call to McCarthy, informing him of the order he had issued, Stevens described the senator's treatment of Zwicker as "outrageous." He told McCarthy: "I'm not going to stand for having Army officers pushed around." Stevens added, if McCarthy was going to insist on demanding further information about the Peress case, he should call *him* to testify—"but leave my officers alone." The senator replied that he certainly would subpoena Stevens—that he intended to "kick the teeth in of anyone caught coddling communists."

Over the next several days, it seemed that a full-scale confrontation between McCarthy and the Eisenhower administration might be inevitable. But several Republicans, mindful that 1954 was a congressional election year, determined to try to head off the threatened showdown. Republican Senators Mundt and Dirksen persuaded McCarthy and Stevens to join them for a private lunch in a Capitol office on February 24 to try to resolve the disagreement. After a prolonged and heated discussion, Mundt rolled a sheet of paper into a typewriter and began preparing a "memorandum of understanding" to be issued to the press by McCarthy and Stevens.

Four points were included in the memorandum: Stevens would order the army's inspector general to finish an investigation of the Peress case as soon as possible; everyone involved in the promotion and discharge of Peress would be made available for questioning by McCarthy; General Zwicker's return for further questioning by the McCarthy committee would be postponed; and Stevens's scheduled appearance before the committee would be canceled. Although it was not included in the memorandum, there was also a verbal agreement that army officers testifying before McCarthy in the future would be treated more fairly and respectfully than Zwicker had been.

When the memorandum was released to the press, it was widely interpreted as a surrender by Stevens—which McCarthy encouraged.

Stevens, fearing further deterioration of army morale, appealed for support from the White House. Despite his hands-off attitude on the dispute, President Eisenhower asked Senator Dirksen to try to get McCarthy to sign a new statement admitting that he had treated Zwicker unfairly, and suggesting that it might not be necessary to call further witnesses on the Peress case. McCarthy was unwilling to concede anything. A short time later, Stevens appeared at the White House and read a new statement

to the press concerning his luncheon meeting with Mc-
Carthy; he said he had not backed away from his principles, and would not accede to the abuse of army personnel
"under any circumstances, including committee hearings."
White House Press Secretary James Hagerty then told the
newsmen: "On behalf of the president, he has seen the
statement. He approves and endorses it 100 percent."
McCarthy responded by accusing Stevens of making "a
completely false statement."

On March 9, McCarthy received his sharpest criticism
from a fellow Republican, Senator Ralph E. Flanders
of Vermont. In a speech to the Senate, Flanders accused
McCarthy of diverting attention from the real issues of the
day and said: "One must conclude that his is a one-man
party and that its name is 'McCarthyism.' . . . He dons
his war paint. . . . He goes forth to battle, and proudly
returns with the scalp of a pink Army dentist."

At a news conference, Eisenhower praised Flanders's
speech, spoke against McCarthy's investigation of the
army and the Peress case, and went out of his way to
praise General Zwicker, citing his distinguished war
record. McCarthy refused to back down.

Administration officials, convinced that further efforts
to reach an accommodation with McCarthy would be fruit-
less, took the offensive. They released to the McCarthy
committee and the press a thirty-four-page report on the
McCarthy–Roy Cohn efforts to get favored treatment
for G. David Schine. The report, giving precise details,
created a sensation.

With the release of the army report, committee members expressed outrage and called for the firing of Roy
Cohn. McCarthy, denying the army accusations, defended
his own actions and Cohn's, as well as accusing the army

[214]

of trying to "blackmail" him in attempts to get him to drop his Fort Monmouth investigations.

Members of the committee now called for an investigation of the allegations made by the army and by McCarthy. No other Senate committee was willing to undertake the investigation, so there was no choice but to carry it out by itself. The hearings, with Senator Mundt moved up to temporary chairman of the committee, became a national televised spectacle. As many as 20,000,000 Americans sat glued to their sets on some days to view angry clashes between McCarthy and his adversaries—which stretched over three months.

On August 31, 1954, the Republican and Democratic members issued separate reports on the investigation. Both reports were critical of various aspects of the behavior of McCarthy, Cohn, and army officials—but rather inconclusive. The Republicans tended to stress insufficient evidence, whereas the Democrats stressed inexcusable actions. Ultimately McCarthy resumed chairmanship of his committee, but under further pressure from both Democratic and Republican members, Roy Cohn resigned.

Following this episode, McCarthy faced the most serious challenge to his political career. Senator Ralph Flanders introduced a resolution calling on the entire Senate to censure McCarthy. Such a resolution was extremely rare. After three days of debate, the Senate voted 75 to 12 to empower Vice-President Nixon, as the chamber's presiding officer, to appoint a special committee to consider the censure resolution. Nixon named a committee of six, of which Senator Arthur Watkins of Utah was chairman.

The committee considered various charges against

McCarthy and eventually broke them down into five categories. The first concerned financial matters and alleged misuse of funds; the second, his dealings with other senators and Senate committees, and his refusal to cooperate with committees investigating him; the third, allegations that he influenced government employees to break the law, and to give him secret information; the fourth, his actual acceptance of such information; and the fifth, his alleged mistreatment of witnesses, particularly General Zwicker.

During September 1954, the committee conducted nine public hearings. McCarthy made numerous efforts to disrupt the proceedings, but on September 27 the Watkins committee filed a unanimous report that recommended censure of McCarthy on two counts, which covered the five categories of charges. The detailed report was sent to the full Senate for consideration, and the Senate debate began on November 10 and continued sporadically for nearly three weeks.

Meanwhile, McCarthy had launched a series of attacks on members of the Watkins committee, calling them "unwitting handmaidens" of the Communist Party, "stupid," and "cowardly"; he also claimed that the entire Senate, in its debate over the Watkins report, was engaged in a "lynch party." On December 2, the censure resolution was passed by a Senate vote of 67 to 22. Among the 67 votes for the resolution, 22 were cast by McCarthy's fellow Republicans. When asked for a comment, McCarthy said: "Well, it wasn't exactly a vote of confidence."

The flippancy of the remark failed to convey the seriousness of McCarthy's defeat. The overwhelming vote by his colleagues to condemn him was a blow from which he would never recover. With startling suddenness, he ceased to be an important political force in American life, and his role as the holy terror of Capitol Hill was at an end. He made periodic attempts to regain the limelight, but the press virtually ignored him. He was no longer in demand as a public speaker, nor did other politicians call upon him to support their campaigns. President Eisenhower's office announced that he would no longer be welcome at White House social events.

McCarthy fell into poor health, and during 1956 and early 1957 he was in and out of hospitals. On May 2, 1957, he died at Bethesda Naval Hospital in Maryland of what was described as "acute hepatitic infection."

The havoc McCarthy left in his wake, was enormous. Lives and reputations had been ruined. Valuable government programs had been disrupted. Careers of effective public servants had been reduced to shambles. And an aura of general suspicion—from which no man or woman was safe—was spread throughout the nation.

All of this did not end when McCarthy died. Despite the fact that he had been personally discredited in his latter years, the era of McCarthyism continued—long after he had passed from the scene.

SOURCES AND SUPPLEMENTARY READING

Personal accounts of the late President Dwight D. Eisenhower's decision to move against Senator McCarthy are provided in Eisenhower's memoirs, *The White House Years: Mandate for Change* (Doubleday, 1963), and in books by two of his aides: *Firsthand Report* by Sherman Adams (Harper and Brothers, 1961) and *The Ordeal of Power* by Emmet John Hughes (Atheneum, 1963).

Newspapers and magazines devoted almost unprecedented space to the running feud between McCarthy and army officials. As a newspaper reporter during that period, I made my own contributions to that abundant coverage. Both my own stories and those of other journalists were helpful to me in reconstructing the events. Former Senator Charles E. Potter's *Days of Shame*, Richard H. Rovere's *Senator Joe McCarthy*, Fred J. Cook's *The Nightmare Decade*, and Lately Thomas's *When Even Angels Wept* were also useful.

12
★ ★ ★

The House Committee
Rises Again

Even before Senator Joseph McCarthy's death, during the period when his career was in decline, others moved to perpetuate the witch hunt as a staple of American political life. Members of the House Un-American Activities Committee, who had taken a back seat to McCarthy throughout his years of power, were among those eagerly grasping for leadership of the witch-hunt movement.

By 1955, Democratic Congressman Francis E. Walter of Pennsylvania had become chairman of HUAC. A banker, Walter had served in the House since 1932. His chief claim to fame before assuming the committee chairmanship had been that he had co-authored the controversial Walter-McCarran Act of 1952—which sharply restricted immigration into the United States. He often expressed suspicion of foreign-born groups, referring to their members derogatorily as "hyphenated Americans." He described immigration policies as "security" matters that should not be handled in a "fraudulently humane" manner. And in a House speech on

[219]

current immigrants to the United States, he said: "I don't think these people are the kind of people our ancestors were."

Walter's distrust of the foreign-born was matched by his suspicion of those whose political views differed from his own, which were basically conservative. This suspicion frequently found expression in his leadership of the committee.

One of the first investigations he directed as chairman was aimed at the Fund for the Republic—a private foundation that often supported liberal causes and opposed the aims of the commitee. The Fund for the Republic was headed by Robert M. Hutchins, former president of the University of Chicago. It was founded in 1951 to work toward "the elimination of restrictions on freedom of thought, inquiry and expression in the United States." Among the projects it had sponsored were a study of congressional investigating committees, programs aimed at fostering racial integration, and a study of blacklisting in the entertainment industry. It had also made a $5,000 grant to a Quaker group in Pennsylvania that had hired a librarian accused of being a former communist.

Walter, in opening the investigation of the fund, said its purpose would be to answer the question: "Is this foundation, with its vast reservoir of funds and power, a friend or foe in the nation's death struggle against the communist conspiracy?" Although another House committee actually was responsible for investigating foundations, Walter brushed aside complaints that his committee had no jurisdiction to conduct the inquiry into the Fund.

He was particularly upset by the Fund's study of blacklisting and its $5,000 grant to the Pennsylvania Quaker group. He and the committee's staff director, Richard

Arens, tried to discredit the blacklisting report that had been prepared under the direction of John Cogley, former executive editor of the liberal Catholic publication *Commonweal*. Walter and Arens, contending that there had never been any such thing as a blacklist, attempted to show that some of those who assisted Cogley in the study had questionable backgrounds.

Other attempts by the committee to discredit the blacklisting report were equally unconvincing. Nonetheless, Walter concluded hearings on the subject by claiming that the report "is a partisan, biased attack on all persons and organizations who are sincerely and patriotically concerned in ridding the movie industry and radio and television of communists and communist sympathizers."

He next turned to the question of the grant to the Quaker group in Plymouth, Pennsylvania. Testimony disclosed that the Quaker group, known as the Plymouth Monthly Meeting, had hired Mrs. Mary Knowles as a librarian upon learning that she was encountering problems finding work after being identified as a former communist by a one-time undercover agent. Before being hired, Mrs. Knowles assured the group that in 1947 she had severed all ties with alleged subversive organizations. Still, her employment stirred a controversy in the community. As a result, several financial contributors to the library withdrew their donations. To make up for the shortage of money in the library budget—and demonstrate its support for the Quaker group's willingness to champion an unpopular cause—the Fund for the Republic donated the $5,000. The Un-American Activities Committee failed to show there was anything sinister about the contribution, and seemed satisfied to produce testimony that the donation created further controversy in Plymouth.

Officials of the Fund demanded that the committee permit them to testify about the full scope of their work. Walter promised to do so, but reneged—after reaping a sufficient amount of publicity.

In 1956, Walter allowed his committee's files to be misused by a southern congressman seeking to smear respected civil-rights leaders. In advance of a large civil-rights demonstration in Washington, Walter opened the committee's files to Democratic Congressman E. C. Gathings of Arkansas. Using excerpts from the files, Gathings read into the *Congressional Record* claims that leaders of the National Association for the Advancement of Colored People—including the organization's highly respected executive secretary, Roy Wilkins, and Ralph Bunche, a Nobel Peace Prize winner who was undersecretary general of the United Nations—had subversive backgrounds.

The claims were misleading. Over the years, the NAACP leaders had occasionally supported causes that had also been backed by members of alleged subversive organizations. They had not been members of such organizations themselves and had taken no part in purportedly subversive activities. But their names had been linked in the Un-American Activities Committee files with those of alleged subversives. Gathings succeeded in persuading some uninformed persons that his charges must be true because "they came straight out of the files." The allegations, which were backed by other southern congressmen, were used to try to discredit the civil-rights demonstration. Walter and other members of the Un-American Activities Committee professed to see nothing wrong with such use of their files.

That same year, so-called "freedom fighters" tried

to overthrow the communist government in Hungary. Their attempted revolution was thwarted when the Soviet Union, in a massive and bloody display of military might, sent troops to crush the poorly armed "freedom fighters." Many American communists became disillusioned over the brutality and oppression exhibited by the Russians and quit the Communist Party in disgust. The party reached its lowest ebb in decades, both in membership and in influence.

But Walter and his colleagues—apparently fearful that public recognition of the party's diminished strength would make it appear their committee was no longer necessary— spread the word that the communists were actually more dangerous than ever. They said that the party was not really weakened, that it had merely gone underground and therefore would be much harder to combat.

Still, some of the targets the committee chose for subsequent investigations did not seem to pose much of a threat to the nation's security. In early 1957, for example, there was an investigation of about thirty musicians in New York who were accused of having subversive backgrounds. The hearings gave every appearance of being devoted to exposure for exposure's sake. Many of the witnesses, as expected, pleaded the Fifth Amendment, and then encountered major problems in finding work.

Later, the committee carried out an equally unproductive investigation of the selection of works of art sent to represent the United States at an exhibit in the Soviet Union. Walter claimed the collection included works by more than twenty artists with communist-front affiliations. Also, he did not like the types of art chosen for the exhibit. But the question of whether the committee feared the collection might somehow help "communize" the Rus-

[223]

sian people, who already had a communist government and culture, was neither asked nor answered during the committee hearings.

Not only the legislative branch of government but the executive branch as well was involved in conducting political witch hunts during this period. President Eisenhower, who had been reelected in 1956, expanded President Truman's loyalty-review boards to a complex network of checks and rechecks on persons employed by the government or by private industries awarded government contracts.

During the 1950s, almost 10,000,000 Americans were subject to clearance by such boards in order to obtain or keep their jobs. They included 2,500,000 federal employees, 3,500,000 members of the armed forces, 3,000,000 workers in private industry, 500,000 merchant seamen and port workers, and 100,000 whose work was under the supervision of the Atomic Energy Commission.

The Fund for the Republic conducted an intensive study of loyalty-board programs that disclosed numerous cases in which injustices had been inflicted in the name of protecting national security. To guard the victims against further harassment by neighbors and prospective employers, the study did not divulge their names—but it was crammed with specific details about typical case histories.

Often, the general public had no idea of the harm being done to innocent individuals in such cases. The loyalty investigations were conducted in secret. And the victims, in order to spare themselves further embarrassment, frequently preferred suffering in silence to making public the injustices done to them. But occasionally a loyalty case would wind up in the courts, and the citizenry would be given a glimpse of the witch-hunt philosophy at work in the government security program.

While such cases indicated the executive branch was inflicting frequent abuses on innocent persons in the name of national security, some critics—led by members of the House Un-American Activities Committee—charged that the government still was not doing enough to protect the country against subversion. Loyalty programs notwithstanding, they accused the Eisenhower administration with the old charge of being "soft on communism."

The Un-American Activities Committee became irate, for example, over a government decision made in February 1960. It involved a training manual that had been issued to cadets at Lackland Air Force Base in Texas. The manual, prepared by an officer on the base, claimed that communists had infiltrated American churches. Its information was based largely on the discredited writings of J. B. Matthews, the former aide to the McCarthy committee.

When Air Force Secretary Dudley Sharp learned of the manual's existence, he immediately ordered it withdrawn and apologized for the fact that it had been distributed in the first place. Not so Congressman Walter and his colleagues. They summoned Secretary Sharp to a hearing and demanded to know why the manual had been withdrawn.

Sharp said he did not feel it was the business of the air force to concern itself with whether communists had infiltrated the churches, and he refused to order the manuals reissued. Walter satisfied himself by telling the press that Sharp had not disputed the accuracy of the information contained in the manual.

Three months later, the committee became involved in one of the most controversial episodes in its history—one that would erupt into violence. The committee had decided to investigate alleged subversion among teachers in California. It subpoenaed 110 teachers to appear at scheduled hearings in San Francisco. Committee officials leaked the names of the teachers—plus brief biographies of each of them and summaries of the allegations—to the press.

Articles containing unproved charges against the teachers appeared in various newspapers in advance of the scheduled hearings. Chairman Walter then unexpectedly postponed the hearings—thus denying the teachers a forum in which to defend themselves. Walter claimed further investigation was needed before the hearings could take place.

The committee's handling of the affair touched off a wave of criticism. The California Democratic Council assailed the committee's actions and urged members of California's delegation in Congress to "employ all means at their disposal . . . to prevent any further maligning of the reputations of California citizens." The California Teachers Association, the California Federation of Labor, and other organizations joined in protesting the committee's tactics.

Chairman Walter responded to all this by announcing that the committee would send dossiers on the 110 teachers to their respective school boards, so that appropriate action might be taken against them. Such action was clearly outside the province of a congressional committee. Moreover, the dossiers contained no proof of wrongdoing —merely undocumented allegations and, in many cases, the lowest form of gossip. Much of the information in the dossiers was attributed to unidentified persons and was at least ten years old.

The American Civil Liberties Union filed suit to prevent the committee from turning the dossiers over to the local school boards. In an attempt to get around the suit, the committee gave the files to the California education superintendent. But the state attorney general, after studying the dossiers, advised the education superintendent that they were worthless as evidence. Despite the fact that a court order based on the ACLU suit barred it from doing so, the committee had copies of the dossiers delivered to the local school boards. Six of the teachers involved were shortly fired.

In May 1960, the committee scheduled hearings in San Francisco—not into the allegations against the teachers but into purported operations of the Communist Party in northern California. By that time, resentment against the committee was running high in California. Numerous groups had banded together to protest the committee's operations and demand that the committee be abolished. Among those participating in the protest were students and faculty members at the University of California, San Francisco State College, Stanford University, and San Jose State College; members of the Central Labor Councils of five northern California counties; and officials of various religious organizations.

In an attempt to blunt the effect of the protests and assure that the hearings at the San Francisco City Hall would be played out before a friendly audience, the committee contrived a plan to pack the hearing room with its supporters. A committee investigator, William Wheeler, issued white admission tickets to large groups of invited guests from right-wing "patriotic" organizations that staunchly backed the committee. Those holding the white tickets were guaranteed entry to the hearing room, while many other persons who stood in line for hours were denied admission. Only a few seats were available for persons who did not have white tickets.

When the hearings opened on May 12, more than a thousand persons conducted a protest demonstration on downtown San Francisco streets. Several hundred others paraded around City Hall itself, then lined up outside the hearing room and demanded admission—but of course they didn't have white tickets.

Inside, before its friendly audience, the committee devoted most of its time to hearing two friendly witnesses, former communists Karl Prussion and Barbara Hartle. The witnesses told the committee members what they apparently wanted to hear—that the Communist Party was far from dead and, in fact, posed a greater danger than ever. As Prussion put it: "Never before in the history of the Communist Party of the United States has the situation been more critical for our democratic form of government."

While the hearings were recessed for lunch, a mass rally in opposition to the committee, organized by a student group, took place in San Francisco's Union Square. California Assemblyman Philip Burton told the crowd: "No legislative committee should have the power to place people in the calumny of the community without going through due process of law. I am looking forward to the day when . . . [Congress] will abolish this committee." An Episcopal clergyman, the Reverend Richard Byfield, said: "These unjustly conducted hearings not only damage individuals but also our society."

The next morning, the hearings began their second

day—but the white-ticket system was used again and most of the seats were given to friends of the committee.

During the lunch recess, San Francisco Sheriff Matthew Carberry—who was in charge of maintaining order at the hearings—told the students that he would try to arrange admission on a first-come, first-served basis if they would refrain from further protests. The students agreed, but said they would resume shouting if the restrictive seating policy were continued. When the afternoon session began, holders of white tickets were again given preference, and only eight students were allowed inside. The students outside the hearing room began shouting: "We're still here!"

Suddenly, policemen started unrolling high-pressure fire hoses in the corridors. The students sat down in the City Hall rotunda. The police turned on the hoses and sent powerful sprays of water rushing at the students. Committee investigator William Wheeler urged the officers to direct the hoses first one way, then another—picking out particular students he wanted sprayed.

The hoses were turned off and the policemen began clubbing the students with night sticks, then dragging them down a flight of marble stairs. Many students banged their heads and spines on the steps as they were pulled along. Several were kicked in the face by officers. Others were beaten about their heads and bodies. The violence continued for about a half hour.

All told, sixty-four students were arrested on charges of disturbing the peace, inciting to riot, and resisting arrest. The police claimed their action against the students had been necessary because one student had jumped over a barricade, assaulted an officer, and led a charge on the hearing-room door. But this version was disputed by the students, who said the police had begun their assault without provocation. When the student accused of jumping over the barricade came to trial, he was found not guilty. The charges against the other sixty-three students were found by a judge to be so flimsy that he dismissed them without bringing them to trial.

Nonetheless, members of the Un-American Activities Committee defended the police actions and claimed the disturbances resulted from a communist plot. Republican Congressman Gordon Scherer of Ohio, for example, said the student protests were "clearly planned at the highest communist levels." "Nobody incited us, nobody misguided us," the students said in a joint statement. "We were led by our own convictions, and we still stand firmly by them."

On the day after the disturbances, the committee wound up its San Francisco hearings. More than 5,000 students demonstrated outside City Hall in protest. Congressman Scherer called them "victims of this despicable propaganda plot"—but again failed to show that any plot existed.

Two days after leaving San Francisco, the committee subpoenaed all news films of the demonstrations and disturbances shot by local television stations. The stations, assuming the committee merely wanted the films for its files, surrendered them. The committee then turned the films over to a commercial Washington movie studio, which used them to piece together a forty-five-minute propaganda film, *Operation Abolition*.

Pieces of film were spliced together in improper sequence that gave misleading impressions. Pictures of alleged communists who had not even been present at the time of the disturbances were also included. The narration, by a committee aide, was full of references to "communist agitators" and "top communist operators especially trained in incitement to riot." All of this was introduced by a statement from Chairman Walter: "During the next few minutes you will see revealed the long-time classic communist tactic in which a relatively few well-trained, hard-core communist agents are able to incite and use noncommunist sympathizers to perform the dirty work of the Communist Party."

The commercial film studio that put the picture together then sold copies of the movie for $100 each to more than 2,000 television stations and private organizations for viewing throughout the country. The showings touched off numerous protests. Critics of the committee, in addition to assailing the distortions in the film, charged that the committee had no authority to engage in propaganda activities. They also accused the committee of impropriety for permitting a private company, the film studio, to make profits on what was supposedly a congressional document. The ACLU of Northern California, in an attempt to counter the impressions given by *Operation Abolition*, used copies of the film footage shot by San Francisco television stations to produce a movie entitled *Operation Correction*. It exposed the numerous errors and distortions in the committee film, but never achieved distribution so wide as that of *Operation Abolition*.

The furor over the San Francisco hearings and *Operation Abolition* damaged the committee's already-sagging prestige, and its activities faded from the front pages.

Meanwhile, in November 1960, Democratic Senator John F. Kennedy of Massachusetts defeated Vice-President Richard Nixon in the race for president. After he assumed

[231]

the presidency the following January, Kennedy took steps to eliminate abuses in the government loyalty program. He removed from positions in the executive branch officials who had been accused of conducting witch hunts. He reduced the authority of government agencies, such as the Subversive Activities Control Board, to take arbitrary action against persons suspected of holding unpopular beliefs. He and his brother, Attorney General Robert F. Kennedy, liberalized Justice Department procedures for dealing with alleged subversion.

There were some who assumed that the witch-hunt movement in the United States was coming to an end. But as future events were to show, they were mistaken.

SOURCES AND SUPPLEMENTARY READING

The background of Congressman Francis E. Walter and the record of his service as chairman of the House Un-American Activities Committee are described in detail in Frank J. Donner's *The Un-Americans* and in Walter Goodman's *The Committee.*

Donner's book is particularly useful in examining the committee's investigation of alleged subversion among California teachers. If a reader takes into account Donner's admitted bias against the committee and compensates for it, he can obtain a great deal of valuable information from *The Un-Americans*—not only about the California investigation but other subjects as well.

Fred J. Cook's *The Nightmare Decade* contains a lengthy discussion of the Fund for the Republic's study of government loyalty-board programs.

13

★ ★ ★

Witch Hunters
Take On the Peace Movement

Each time the witch-hunt movement seemed to run out of steam and reach the verge of its death throes, it somehow revived. Even if the Kennedy administration showed no inclination to hunt for communists under every bed, congressional witch hunters could always be counted upon to snap out of their periodic lethargy and claim the discovery of some new threat to the nation's security.

During 1961 and most of 1962, for example, little was heard from the House Un-American Activities Committee. But then in December 1962, the committee blazed back into the headlines with a controversial investigation of a group of women—mostly housewives—banded together in an organization known as Women Strike for Peace.

The organization had been founded in the fall of 1961 at the instigation of Mrs. Dagmar Wilson, an illustrator of children's books who lived in Washington, D.C. Its chief efforts were devoted to trying to bring about a ban on the testing of nuclear bombs. Some scientists had been warning that radioactive fallout resulting from nuclear tests could be extremely dangerous, especially to small children.

President Kennedy advocated negotiation of a treaty with the Soviet Union banning further nuclear tests in the atmosphere. But such an agreement was opposed by many congressmen, including members of the Un-American Activities Committee, who contended (among other things) that it would represent a softening of the American position toward communism. While American and Russian diplomats tried to work out the terms of a proposed agreement, both countries voluntarily refrained from conducting nuclear tests for a time. Shortly before the formation of Women Strike for Peace, however, the Soviet Union resumed testing; the United States followed suit in the spring of 1962.

Women Strike for Peace conducted numerous demonstrations against the resumption of the tests and in favor of a test-ban treaty. Thousands of housewives across the country participated in such demonstrations in scores of cities. Almost 2,000 women went to Washington to lobby for their cause on Capitol Hill and to picket outside the White House. Others picketed outside the United Nations building in New York.

It was against this background that the committee launched its investigation into Women Strike for Peace. The committee tried to show that the organization, rather than being made up merely of well-meaning housewives, actually was dominated by communists. It began its hearings by calling as witnesses members of other peace groups—having nothing to do with Women Strike for Peace —who had been accused of having subversive backgrounds.

The committee then called several members of Women Strike for Peace from the New York area. Democratic

Congressman Clyde Doyle of California ventured the opinion that being a member of a peace movement did not automatically make a person a communist, but the impression was left that there was something suspicious about advocating peace.

When Mrs. Dagmar Wilson was called to the witness chair, Committee Counsel Alfred Nittle emphasized that the committee had no evidence she was a communist or even a communist sympathizer. But he tried to show that she had allowed communists to control the organization. Mrs. Wilson denied the allegation, but said that Women Strike for Peace was a loosely organized group whose rules made no provision for barring any would-be member —no matter what her political beliefs.

Throughout the hearings, the committee room was filled with housewives, many of them carrying babies in their arms. As each witness was summoned to testify, she was handed a bouquet by one of her supporters in the audience. The overall effect was to open the committee to ridicule. Moreover, the proposed test-ban treaty supported by the women was also advocated by President Kennedy. Was the committee suggesting that the president, too, was part of a plot? Such questions, raised by critics of the investigation but never answered, helped leave the impression that the committee had stubbed its toe badly in conducting the hearings.

In 1963, the United States and the Soviet Union reached agreement on a limited test-ban treaty—much to the delight of Women Strike for Peace and to the displeasure of members of the Un-American Activities Committee.

Congressman Walter died of leukemia in May 1963, and Democratic Congressman Edwin Willis of Louisiana succeeded him as chairman of the committee. Willis, who had served seven terms in the House, was known as a political conservative and an outspoken defender of racial segregation. Under his leadership, the committee followed policies set by his predecessors and continued to keep close watch over the activities of the peace movement.

After President Kennedy had been assassinated on November 22, 1963, he had been succeeded in office by Vice-President Lyndon B. Johnson. In the 1964 national election, Johnson had won his own four-year term as president. During his presidency, the United States greatly escalated its involvement in the Vietnam War. The peace movement likewise escalated and became increasingly vocal. It was a time of major ferment in the country— of countless street demonstrations and other protests. Many thousands of persons, including contingents from civil-rights organizations and the so-called "New Left," joined the peace movement. There is no question that some members of communist and communist-front groups became active in the movement, but their numbers were small in relation to those of the noncommunists involved. But by the committee standards, it seemed, opposition to the war in itself represented grounds for suspicion.

A favorite committee tactic was to subpoena as witnesses members of the most radical elements of the peace movement—leaving the public with the impression that such witnesses were typical, rather than representative of a small minority within the movement. Tumultuous hearings often resulted. Among the most boisterous were those conducted by the committee in Washington in August 1966.

The hearings concerned the antiwar activities of members of a splinter group in the Progressive Labor Party

(PL)—a group that supported the Maoist, rather than the Soviet, brand of communism. Demonstrators packed the hearing room, booing and hissing committee members and making themselves generally disruptive. About fifty of them were expelled from the hearings by federal marshals. An attorney for some of the witnesses, Arthur Kinoy, also was expelled when he objected strenuously to committee procedures.

For once, however, the committee was not confronted with witnesses who pleaded the Fifth Amendment when asked whether they were communists. The PL members were only too pleased to declare their advocacy of communism. In doing so, they tried to use the hearings as a forum for describing at length their political philosophies and what they regarded as the failings of the American system. Such declarations led to frequent clashes with members and staff aides of the committee. And while refraining from pleading the Fifth Amendment, several witnesses challenged the committee's right to conduct the investigation.

Among them was Richard Mark Rhoads of the New York PL.

Committee Counsel Alfred Nittle began the questioning by asking Rhoads the extent of his education, to which Rhoads eventually replied: "In the last few years I have been attending what you might call a school of life known as the United States." In reply to the question "Are you presently the editor of *Free Student* [a PL publication]?" Rhoads replied: "*Free Student* is an anti-imperialist newspaper . . ."—but was not allowed to finish his speech. When he was asked the objectives of the Progressive Labor Party, Rhoads read from the preamble of the party's constitution, which stated in part:

[237]

We resolve to build a revolutionary movement with the participation and support of millions of working men and women as well as those students, artists and intellectuals who will join the working class to end the profit system which breeds . . . fears and troubles. With such a movement, we will build a socialist U.S.A., with all power in the hands of the working people and their allies.

Chairman Pool then questioned Rhoads:

POOL: Do you advocate the overthrow of the United States government by force and violence?

RHOADS: You gentlemen have some nerve to use "violence" when you are talking about what *we* advocate, because the United States government is the prime user of violence against the people of the United States. . . .

Two days later, the committee called to the witness chair Steven Cherkoss, a student organizer for the Progressive Labor Party from Berkeley, California. He testified without a lawyer because his attorney, along with those for several other witnesses, had refused to appear before the committee in protest of the expulsion from the hearings of lawyer Arthur Kinoy. Cherkoss explained:

You have deprived me of the lawyer of my choice, and I do not wish to be represented by any other lawyer. I could not have confidence in any lawyer who would appear at this time under the circumstances which you, as representatives of a government that is committing war crimes, have created in this kangaroo court. . . .

[238]

Before answering any questions, Cherkoss would make objections and state his opposition to "racist HUAC . . . a circus committee of coward yellow-bellies . . . [who] hope this witch hunt will frighten the massive antiwar movement into passivity. . . ." Pool interrupted and asked Cherkoss if he was a communist. Cherkoss replied: "I am going to finish this statement, one more paragraph, and then I will answer the questions."

In response to Cherkoss's statements about the committee and the United States government, the questioning continued, and Nittle finally said:

> NITTLE: . . . it is the committee's information that you are a West Coast student organizer for the Progressive Labor Party and that you also served as a West Coast spokesman of its front organization, the May Second Movement—
>
> CHERKOSS: The only front I know of here is the front of the CIA for U.S. imperialism. Let us talk about fronts. Let us talk about fronts this government has set up internationally to suppress the people throughout the world. . . .
>
> POOL: You are excused. Step down.

With that, a uniformed policeman led Cherkoss away. A short time later, Congressman Pool abruptly called the hearings to a halt without even summoning to the witness chair several others who had been subpoenaed. "We have the information we set out to obtain," Pool said. "We see no need to continue the investigative phase of this hearing. All witnesses against whom subpoenas are still outstanding are hereby excused from their subpoenas."

In short, the hearings had already served their purpose.

[239]

The Progressive Labor Party witnesses, in filling the hearing record with their vitriolic propaganda statements, had played into the hands of the committee. Members of the committee were now able to point to the inflammatory testimony of these few witnesses—admitted communists —and use it to try to discredit the entire peace movement.

They did so with relish. Committee Chairman Willis, for example, charged that "communist organizations and their adherents . . . have been the originating and guiding force in the major demonstrations." He provided no evidence to support such an assessment, but many Americans were left with the impression that communists dominated the peace movement.

To a limited extent at least, the executive branch of the Johnson administration also used witch-hunt techniques in attempts to tarnish the reputation of the peace movement. A typical example occurred shortly after thousands of demonstrators conducted an antiwar protest outside the Pentagon in October 1967. A few communists apparently took part, but they were far outnumbered by noncommunists. Among the demonstrators were large contingents of highly respected Americans—including author Norman Mailer, poet Robert Lowell, literary critic Dwight Macdonald, and the noted pediatrician Dr. Benjamin Spock.

President Johnson, who was highly sensitive about criticism of his Vietnam War policy, summoned a group of congressmen to a White House meeting a short time after the Pentagon demonstration. He read them a report that claimed the demonstration had been organized on orders from Hanoi, the capital of communist North Vietnam. The congressmen then emerged from the White House and told newsmen about the report. Republican

Representative Frank T. Bow of Ohio, for example, said: "There's no question at all in my mind, after what I heard the president read, that the demonstration was conceived and directed from Hanoi."

Johnson refused to release the report or otherwise document his allegation, saying that to do so might touch off a "McCarthyist witch hunt." But a witch hunt was precisely what he had created by leaking the accusation to the public.

Other actions taken by the executive branch during Johnson's presidency also demonstrated the adoption of witch-hunt tactics. It was during Johnson's term that the government launched a program directly disregarding the long-standing American tradition that military authorities should refrain from investigating civilians' political activities.

In February 1968, the army issued orders to intelligence officers to put under surveillance certain civilians involved in peace and civil-rights groups. The document containing the orders was known as "the intelligence annex of the army's civil-disturbance plan." The intelligence annex made an assumption that civilians involved in such organizations should be equated with subversive conspirators. The army conducted extensive secret investigations of such groups, and civilian members were shadowed by army investigators. In some cases, electronic eavesdropping devices were used to listen in on their conversations. Army undercover agents infiltrated the groups. Dossiers based on reports of such activities were used to compile an army blacklist of so-called agitators."

Details of the army program were disclosed in an investigation carried out by the Senate Subcommittee on Constitutional Rights, headed by Democratic Senator Sam

Ervin of North Carolina. During the hearings, army officials admitted they could not substantiate their allegations.

In April 1968, during and after the urban riots touched off by Martin Luther King's assassination, high-level meetings at the White House resulted in adoption of new orders to broaden the original army program. The new orders were contained in a document called "the army's civil-disturbance information collection plan." It authorized the army to seek information from more than 300 government agencies on suspected subversions in various civilian organizations, including civil-rights and peace groups. Among the agencies were the CIA, the FBI and other law-enforcement units, the President's Foreign Intelligence Advisory Board, and the National Security Council (which is headed by the president).

Among other things, the new plan called for collection of reports on newspapers, radio or television stations, and "prominent persons who are friendly with the leaders of disturbances and are sympathetic with their plans." It also required reports on the "failure of law-enforcement agencies to properly respond due to indecision, lack of manpower or fear of public reaction." Furthermore, as evidence of alleged subversion, it sought information on groups that might "create, prolong or aggravate racial tensions." Specifically identified as groups supposedly falling into those categories were such civil-rights organizations as the NAACP, the Southern Christian Leadership Conference (headed, until his death, by Dr. King), the Congress of Racial Equality, and the Student Nonviolent Coordinating Committee. The orders directed intelligence officers to gather information on such organizations' finances and memberships. They also asked for assessments of the groups' capabilities and weaknesses.

Congressman Ogden Reid of New York was responsible for bringing some of the army's secret activities to light. He said the disclosure showed "the full extent of the army's pervasive intelligence collection activities during [a period] in which no military or civilian official blew the whistle on these operations." Later developments revealed even more about the extensive scope of the army's investigations of civilians. It was disclosed that at least 1,200 army intelligence agents, working out of 300 offices throughout the country, engaged in such work.

Reports on such investigations were forwarded to the army's Counter-Intelligence Analysis Branch at the Pentagon. It was there that the blacklist of supposed civilian "agitators" was compiled, and a thick two-volume "compendium" titled *Counter-Intelligence Research Project on Persons and Organizations of Civil Disturbance Interest* was written. Much of the information gathered was computerized and stored for future use. In most cases, the persons involved had no idea they were under investigation and thus were provided no means of challenging the accuracy of the information gathered about them.

As mentioned earlier, the FBI aided in conducting such investigations at the time. Documents made public in 1974 revealed that the late FBI Director J. Edgar Hoover had ordered his agents across the country to expose, disrupt, and "otherwise neutralize" a variety of such organizations during the 1960s.

The documents quoted Hoover as saying that a major goal of his campaign was to prevent the rise "of a 'messiah' who could unify and electrify the militant black nationalist movement." A memo from Hoover, dated March 4, 1968, said that the black nationalist leader Malcolm X "might have been such a 'messiah.'" But Malcolm X was assassinated in 1965, leading Hoover to comment in the memo: "He is the martyr of the movement today." The memo mentioned several other persons, whose names were not made public, and said they "all aspire to this position" (of "messiah"). One of them, apparently a reference to Dr. Martin Luther King, Jr., was said by Hoover to be "a very real contender for this position should he abandon his supposed 'obedience' to [non-violence] and embrace black nationalism." This man, Hoover wrote, "has the necessary charisma to be a real threat in this way." A month after Hoover wrote the memo Dr. King was assassinated.

Another memo said that Hoover's campaign against black organizations was being carried out by forty-one FBI field offices throughout the country. The campaign's purpose, the memo said, was to prevent "an effective coalition of black nationalist groups [that] might be the first step toward a real 'Mau Mau' in America, the beginning of a true black revolution." Still another memo outlined what Hoover called a "disruptive-disinformation program" against the Black Panther Party.

Nowhere did Hoover or any other government official cite any legal authority for the FBI to conduct such activities. But over the years, the FBI has remained remarkably free of criticism—particularly from members of the legislative and executive branches of government. Thus, release of the documents revealing the FBI's secret activities created scarcely a ripple of official complaint.

One investigation that involved personnel from a wide

variety of government agencies—including the army, the FBI and other federal law-enforcement units, local police, and eventually the House Un-American Activities Committee—concerned the demonstrations and disruptions at the 1968 Democratic National Convention in Chicago. A large coalition of protest groups had banded together in advance of the convention to demonstrate against the policies of the administration, especially the Vietnam War policy.

In the forefront of the groups planning the protests was the National Mobilization Committee to End the War in Vietnam. The committee, which had previously organized numerous antiwar demonstrations, was headed by David Dellinger, editor of a publication called *Liberation*. Cooperating closely with Dellinger were such well-known radicals as Rennie Davis, head of the Center for Radical Research; Tom Hayden, a former president of Students for a Democratic Society; and Abbie Hoffman and Jerry Rubin, leaders of the Youth International Party, commonly known as the Yippies.

As is now well known, there was substantial violence in Chicago. The violence received such wide publicity that there is no need to dwell on it at length here. Thousands of demonstrators swarmed through the streets. Chicago police, in attempting to disband them, went on club-swinging forays into the throngs of protesters. All told, 668 persons were arrested, and 1,025 civilians and 192 policemen were injured in the resulting tumult.

The National Commission on the Causes and Prevention of Violence, appointed by President Johnson, assigned a study team to investigate the disturbances. The major finding in the team's report was that a "police riot" had erupted in Chicago, but demonstrators were not absolved of blame. The report noted that "the Chicago police were the targets of mounting provocation by both word and act." But the report emphasized: "Despite the presence of some revolutionaries, the vast majority of the demonstrators were intent on expressing by peaceful means their dissent either from society generally or from the administration's policies in Vietnam."

As a result of an investigation by the FBI and other law-enforcement agencies, seven leaders of the protest groups—including David Dellinger, Rennie Davis, Tom Hayden, Abbie Hoffman, and Jerry Rubin—were indicted on charges of violating a 1968 federal antiriot law. A jury eventually found all of them not guilty of conspiracy, but convicted Dellinger, Davis, Hayden, Hoffman, and Rubin of crossing state lines to incite a riot. The convictions, however, were later reversed by an appeals court.

Meanwhile, the House Un-American Activities Committee had launched its own investigation. Within two weeks after the Democratic convention, the committee had passed a resolution appointing a subcommittee to investigate the violence. The resolution claimed the committee had "evidence . . . that communist, pro-communist and other cooperating subversive elements" had deliberately planned acts of violence in Chicago—thus proclaiming its position even in advance of beginning the investigation.

The subcommittee, headed by Democratic Congressman Richard Ichord of Missouri, opened public hearings on October 1, 1968. It called as its first witness a committee investigator, James L. Gallagher, who proceeded to enter into the record broad-scale charges of subversion against those who had taken part in the Chicago demonstrations. "The Communist Party, along with several rival communist groups, was deeply involved in the advance preparation made for Chicago," Gallagher testified. Of course, such testimony by a committee staffer amounted to the committee's telling itself what it wanted to hear. It was a standard tactic.

Gallagher was followed to the witness chair by two members of the Chicago Police Department special unit assigned to investigate alleged subversives. Lieutenant Joseph J. Healy and Sergeant Joseph Grubisic. They told of planting undercover informers inside various organizations involved in the Chicago demonstrations. Like Gallagher, they blamed subversives for the disturbances.

The next witness was Robert L. Pierson, an investigator for the district attorney's office in Chicago. He testified that he had posed as a disruptive demonstrator during the Chicago protests in order to gather information for the district attorney's office. Pierson conceded before the subcommittee that he had, indeed, thrown rocks, but claimed he had done so strictly in the line of duty. Members of the subcommittee took pains to congratulate Pierson for his work and to emphasize that they saw nothing improper about his actions.

The subcommittee later called Tom Hayden, Rennie Davis, and David Dellinger as witnesses. The testimony —unlike that in the vitriolic hearings of the 1966 peace movement participants and in the Chicago conspiracy trial itself—had a measured, ironic tone. At one point, Congressman Watson said to Davis: "You have nothing but contempt for this committee. This is [a] fair [statement], isn't it?" And Davis replied: "You men are interesting. I have not found this a complete drag." The basic thrust

[247]

of the questioning concerned the political philosophies of
these three witnesses, and whether or not they wished to
destroy the United States government.

Each of the three answered in relation to his convictions
about what was taking place in the United States concerning civil rights, foreign policy, and the war in Vietnam.
This recent history has been widely discussed and written
about—Tom Hayden wrote a book concerning his trials—
and a much larger segment of the population was aware
of what took place in this hearing than in earlier un-
American activities investigations.

David Dellinger, at the age of fifty-three, was the elder
statesman among the witnesses from the protest movement
called before the subcommittee. A pacifist, he testified
that he had served a prison term during World War II for
refusing to register for the military draft. He was questioned about, among other things, an interview in which
he had been quoted as saying: "There cannot be peace
and tranquility in the United States while the government's foreign policy continues."

In explaining the comment to the committee, Dellinger
said that every effort must be made to deter Americans
from the idea that the United States can "continue business as usual"—and thus uproot people, commit genocide
in Vietnam, in the black community, in Latin America,
or anywhere in the world. He continued:

> We [must] confront [the American people] with the
> reality of the situation and make it impossible for
> us to gorge ourselves on our high standard of living
> and our consumer culture and to dismiss the death
> of American boys and Vietnamese men, women and
> children which is going on daily as long as the war

continues. And it is my intention to do everything I can to make it impossible for the American people to sink back into that kind of apathy and acquiescence.

The subcommittee never came close to showing through the testimony of such witnesses as Hayden, Davis, and Dellinger that subversives had been responsible for the disruptions in Chicago. Still, the subcommittee and the full House Un-American Activities Committee continued to make that claim. It was based chiefly on the testimony of the committee's own employees. In effect, the committee was saying: "You'll just have to take our word for it." Yet, for many Americans, that was enough. As the history of political witch hunts has shown, the mere charge of subversion often is sufficient to receive wide acceptance—no matter how little evidence is offered to support it.

SOURCES AND SUPPLEMENTARY READING

Much of the material in this chapter is based on testimony contained in published transcripts of the House Un-American Activities Committee and in extracts from those transcripts published in Eric Bentley's *Thirty Years of Treason.*

Records of the Senate Subcommittee on Constitutional Rights were useful in studying the army's secret investigations of civil-rights and peace organizations.

Numerous books contain information concerning the protests at the 1968 Democratic National Convention and the witch-hunt activities they generated. My own book, *Confrontation: Politics and Protest* (Delacorte,

1974), contains a chapter describing the events. Other books relating to the protests include *The Conspiracy* by the "Chicago Seven" (Dell, 1969); *The Tales of Hoffman*, edited by Mark L. Levine, George C. McNamee, and Daniel Greenberg (Bantam, 1970); and *Rights in Conflict*, a report to the National Commission on the Causes and Prevention of Violence (1968).

14

★ ★ ★

A Witch Hunter
in the White House

The national election of 1968 saw the American voter
for the first time elect as president a man who had gained
a substantial reputation as a witch hunter. Former Vice-
President Richard Nixon entered the White House after
defeating his Democratic opponent, Vice-President Hubert
H. Humphrey, in the presidential campaign. Not only
had Nixon first attained national recognition as a member of the House Un-American Activities Committee, but
he had also been noted throughout his career for accusing
his political opponents of subversive affiliations or sympathies.

In his first election campaign, for a California congressional seat in 1946, for example, Nixon repeatedly charged
his Democratic opponent, incumbent Representative Jerry
Voorhis, with "following the Moscow line in Congress."
He said Voorhis's voting record "is more socialistic and
communistic than Democratic." As Voorhis later commented: "In most cases I had voted with a majority of

[251]

the House. And, whatever anyone's judgment might have been as to whether I was right or wrong in my votes, to call them 'communistic' was clearly an arrant deception of the voters and a tactic unworthy of a responsible politician." Deceived or not, the voters swept Nixon into office to replace Voorhis.

In 1950, Nixon ran for a California Senate seat against Congresswoman Helen Gahagan Douglas. At the outset of the race, Nixon's campaign manager charged that Mrs. Douglas's record in Congress "discloses the truth about her soft attitude toward communism." Nixon followed that up with a speech claiming that "my opponent is a member of a small clique which joins the notorious communist party-liner, [Congressman] Vito Marcantonio of New York, in voting time after time against measures that are for the security of this country." To promote the idea that Mrs. Douglas was a "pinko," the Nixon forces referred to her as the "Pink Lady." Nixon's campaign. organization distributed 550,000 leaflets—printed on bright pink paper—that purported to show communist sympathies in her voting record. Nixon won the election by a wide margin.

He used similar tactics in his successful vice-presidential campaigns in 1952 and 1956, his unsuccessful presidential race against John F. Kennedy in 1960, and his triumphant 1968 presidential campaign. In all of them, in one manner or another, Nixon tried to picture the Democrats as "soft on communism."

Thus, it was hardly surprising that Nixon, as president, embarked on a broad series of programs aimed at curbing political dissent. Shortly after Nixon took office, his administration announced plans to expand the size and authority of the Justice Department Internal Security

Division—the branch responsible for prosecuting alleged subversives. Nixon appointed to head the division Robert C. Mardian, an extreme conservative known to take a "hard line" on harassing political radicals.

Manpower, funds, and jurisdiction were taken away from other divisions of the Justice Department regarded as more tolerant of political dissent and were centralized in the Internal Security Division. Under Mardian's direction, the division launched broad-scale prosecutions of members of various left-wing groups on charges of violating federal conspiracy laws. Many of these cases were utterly unconvincing to juries and ended in a succession of not-guilty verdicts that proved embarrassing to the administration. (Later, Mardian himself was convicted on a conspiracy charge growing out of his participation in the cover-up of the Watergate scandal.)

Nixon also gave new power to the Subversive Activities Control Board (SACB) that had been created in 1950 by Congress. Protesting that establishment of the agency would require "a great deal of time, effort and money—all to no good end," Truman had vetoed the legislation, but Congress had overridden the veto.

Under the law SACB was supposed to identify "communist-action" and "communist-front" groups and to force them to register with the government and disclose their membership lists and other records. But the Supreme Court ruled that the provision was unconstitutional because it violated the Fifth Amendment's safeguard against forcing anyone to give evidence against himself.

Nonetheless, the SACB remained in existence—conducting sporadic hearings on alleged subversive groups. Its five board members continued drawing annual salaries of $36,000 each. Its budget ran as high as $450,000 a year.

When the Senate Appropriations Committee conducted hearings in 1971 on whether to allocate funds for the SACB, Democratic Senator Allen J. Ellender of Louisiana asked SACB Chairman John W. Mahan what he did with his time.

"I spend some time in the House and Senate trying to correct the law so we can work more effectively," Mahan replied.

"That's not what you're paid to do," Ellender said.

"We do not have enough [work] to fill our time," Mahan conceded.

Meanwhile, President Nixon took his action aimed at pumping new life into the SACB. Nixon issued an executive order empowering the SACB to conduct hearings to help determine which organizations should be classified as subversive by the attorney general. He also proposed giving the SACB the authority to issue subpoenas and to hold uncooperative witnesses in contempt.

Nixon's executive order stirred wide dispute. Melvin L. Wulf, legal director of the American Civil Liberties Union, charged that it was unconstitutional. Democratic Senator Sam Ervin of North Carolina also argued that the executive order was unconstitutional. In addition, he contended that the order would result in violation of the First Amendment guarantee of freedom of association. Ervin said Nixon had "authorized a witch hunt" and exhibited "a fear of freedom, a fear of the American people." The executive order, Ervin said, would "empower the board to brand the organizations and groups specified in it as intellectually or politically dangerous to the established order." In doing so, he continued, it would "place a political stigma" on thousands of persons.

When the Senate voted to appropriate funds for the

SACB, Ervin succeeded in pushing through an amendment barring the agency from using any of the money to implement Nixon's executive order. But the House refused to accept the amendment and, when the issue came up for a second vote in the Senate, Ervin's measure was defeated by a narrow margin. The SACB then put Nixon's plan into operation.

In 1972, Ervin and Democratic Senator William Proxmire of Wisconsin led a drive to put the SACB out of business by cutting off its funds. Proxmire described the SACB as a "boondoggle" and said that in its twenty-two years "the board has not done anything useful." But other senators defended the agency. Democrat John McClellan of Arkansas argued that the SACB should be kept intact because "the threat of subversion is increasing all the time."

It was clear, however, that pressure was mounting in Congress and elsewhere to eliminate the SACB. Nixon finally decided to succumb to the pressure. In 1973, he omitted funds for the agency from his budget, and the SACB went out of existence. A year later, after hearing a Justice Department official admit that the attorney general's list of subversive organizations was "absolutely worthless," Nixon ordered the list abolished. The Justice Department, nonetheless, continues to monitor the activities of individuals and organizations it considers subversive. The department's old Internal Security Division, reorganized as a section of the Criminal Division, maintains jurisdiction over such matters.

Long before the dissolution of the SACB and the abolition of the attorney general's subversive list, the Nixon administration had undertaken new measures designed to ensure continued harassment of left-wing individuals and groups. One such measure, which became extremely controversial when it was finally exposed, involved bringing the Internal Revenue Service (IRS) into the administration's campaign against alleged radicals. Traditionally, the IRS—which administers the federal government's tax programs—is supposed to steer clear of political involvement. Most important, it is expected to refrain from investigating individuals or groups because of their political beliefs.

But that long-standing tradition was set aside by the Nixon administration. In August 1969, on orders from the White House, the IRS secretly established a task force known as "the activist organizations group" to investigate the tax records of purported radical groups. The types of organizations to be investigated were described in a government memorandum as "ideological, militant, subversive, radical or other" groups.

The IRS task force subsequently collected dossiers on more than 10,000 individuals and organizations. Among the groups investigated were the Black Panthers, the Student Nonviolent Coordinating Committee, and Students for a Democratic Society. The IRS tried to force collection of additional taxes from at least forty-three individuals and twenty-six organizations.

In a related action, White House officials drew up a list of persons regarded as Nixon's political enemies—for intended use by the IRS and other federal agencies in further harassment campaigns. The list included 490 names. Among them were ten Democratic senators, including Edward M. Kennedy of Massachusetts, Edmund S. Muskie of Maine, and George McGovern of South Dakota; eighteen House members, twelve of them blacks; other political figures such as John V. Lindsay, then mayor of New York; entertainers such as Barbra Streisand, Paul Newman, and Gregory Peck; numerous newsmen; labor leaders, including Leonard Woodcock, president of the United Auto Workers, and Jerry Wurf, president of the Federal, State, County and Municipal Employees Union; businessmen such as Thomas J. Watson, Jr., board chairman of International Business Machines Corporation, and Maxwell Dane, chairman of the executive committee of the Doyle, Dane and Bernbach advertising agency; and many figures from the nation's academic community.

The criteria used by White House officials in determining who was to be considered an enemy of Nixon were never disclosed. Apparently, some rather obscure persons were placed on the list merely because they had contributed money to the campaign funds of Nixon's opponents.

The existence of the enemies' list was revealed in 1973 in testimony by John Dean, former counsel to Nixon, before a Senate committee investigating the Watergate scandal. Dean said he had been asked in 1971 to prepare a memorandum on use of the list for Nixon's two top aides, H. R. Haldeman and John Ehrlichman: "This memorandum states . . . how can we use the available federal machinery to screw our political enemies." The memo said key members of the White House staff should inform them as to "who they feel we should be giving a hard time."

Disclosure of the existence of the enemies' list brought expressions of outrage from persons both on and off the list. Senator McGovern said: "If ever there was a police-state operation, that's it." Senator Muskie said the list was a "manifestation of the terrible kind of paranoia that afflicts these people." Former Vice-President Humphrey,

[257]

who was not on the list, said: "Some of us see politics as a contest between adversaries. They [White House officials] see it as a war with an enemy to be destroyed."

When the House Judiciary Committee drew up a report recommending Nixon's impeachment in the summer of 1974, it charged him with a wide variety of offenses—many of them falling under the general heading of witch-hunt activities. The committee charged, for example, that Nixon "has repeatedly engaged in conduct violating the constitutional rights of citizens, impairing the due and proper administration of justice and the conduct of lawful inquiries, or contravening the laws governing agencies of the executive branch and the purposes of these agencies."

In another section of its report, the Judiciary Committee accused Nixon of misusing the FBI, the Secret Service, and other federal agencies by ordering them, "in violation or disregard of the constitutional rights of citizens," to use wiretaps and other investigative techniques for improper purposes such as witch-hunting activities. For instance, the committee pointed out, Nixon ordered the FBI to place wiretaps on the home telephones of various administration officials and newsmen who were not suspected of committing any crimes. The wiretaps were intended to lead to identification and punishment of government officials suspected of leaking to the press information that proved embarrassing to the administration.

The committee also noted that Nixon had approved a short-lived plan drawn up by one of his staff assistants, Tom Charles Huston, for using numerous illegal means in attempts to counteract militant protest groups. The so-called "Huston plan" called for federal investigators to take part in burglaries, illegal wiretapping, and monitoring of citizens' mail in order to cope with the supposed threats to national security posed by dissident groups. Huston had admitted in discussions with administration officials that some of the techniques he proposed were "clearly illegal," but had added that they could be "most fruitful." Although Nixon approved implementation of the Huston plan, he changed his mind about two weeks later after being told that FBI Director J. Edgar Hoover considered it improper. Despite its short duration, the mere approval of the plan by Nixon was ruled an impeachable offense by the Judiciary Committee.

The committee also ruled it had been an impeachable offense for Nixon to establish a secret investigative unit known as "the Plumbers" within the White House and to allow the unit to "engage in covert and unlawful activities." These activities included trying to influence improperly the outcome of the trial of Daniel Ellsberg, a former government official, who was eventually found not guilty of charges involving the release to the news media of secret documents known as "The Pentagon Papers." Among other things, Nixon directed one of his aides to leak to the press information seeking to connect one of Ellsberg's lawyers with the Communist Party. In addition, members of "the Plumbers" burglarized the office of Ellsberg's psychiatrist—seeking information from the doctor's files that could be used to discredit Ellsberg. During the harassment campaign against Ellsberg, members of "the Plumbers" and other White House officials enlisted the aid of the CIA in obtaining disguises and false identification papers for their use and a "psychological profile" of Ellsberg.

When it appeared that the charges brought by the Judiciary Committee would be supported by enough members of the House and Senate to bring about his removal from office, President Nixon elected to resign. But allegations of misconduct during his administration—many of them involving witch-hunt activities—continued to arise even after he left office.

In late 1974, for example, the *New York Times* reported that the CIA had conducted a massive domestic intelligence operation in violation of its charter, under the administrations of Nixon and prior presidents. The *Times* charged that the operation had involved, among other things, compilation of dossiers on more than 10,000 Americans who had opposed United States participation in the Vietnam War. By law, the CIA is barred from conducting investigations of such domestic political activities. Nixon's successor as president, Gerald Ford, appointed an eight-member commission to investigate the charges made by the *Times* and other allegations of illegal CIA domestic activities.

The commission, headed by Vice-President Nelson Rockefeller, spent five months conducting its investigation. Then, in June 1975, it issued a 299-page report accusing the CIA of participating in numerous illegal domestic intelligence operations during the administrations of Nixon and prior presidents.

The report charged, for example, that the CIA had carried out widespread investigations of antiwar and civil-rights activists during the late 1960s and early 1970s. Such investigations were prompted by the suspicions of Presidents Johnson and Nixon that American activist groups were financed or otherwise influenced by foreign subversive organizations. When the CIA could find no significant evidence of foreign influence, the Rockefeller commission reported, White House officials demanded that the intelligence agency look harder and "remedy any lack of resources for gathering information."

As a result, the CIA established within its counter-intelligence staff in 1967 a special group, called Operation CHAOS, whose ostensible purpose was to gather information about American dissidents' foreign contacts. The staff of Operation CHAOS eventually accumulated about 13,000 files, including 7,200 on American citizens and organizations.

The commission said the CIA used undercover agents to infiltrate the Washington branches of activist organizations such as Women Strike for Peace and the Congress of Racial Equality. Such infiltration was supposedly intended to keep the CIA informed on plans for demonstrations that might endanger the agency's employees, facilities, or operations. But the Rockefeller commission concluded that the CIA activities "went far beyond steps necessary to protect the agency's own facilities, personnel and operations, exceeded the CIA's statutory authority," and was, therefore, illegal.

Another area in which the commission uncovered illegal operations involved secret interception of mail between Americans and persons in communist countries, particularly the Soviet Union. There were at least four independent CIA programs providing for examination of mail between 1952 and 1973, the commission said. In some cases, the programs involved so-called "mail covers" in which envelopes were examined from the outside and the identities of the writers and intended recipients were copied; in other cases, the envelopes were opened and the contents were photographed. The commission reported that, during 1973 alone, eight CIA employees examined the envelopes of more than 2,300,000 pieces of mail between the United States and the Soviet Union, photographed about 33,000 envelopes, and opened about 8,700. It is illegal for government employees to open mail without search warrants, but the commission said no such warrants were obtained by the CIA.

The commission also reported finding evidence of illegal activities by the CIA in investigating suspected breaches of security by its own employees. Among the activities the commission cited in this field were at least twelve burglaries, thirty-two domestic wiretaps, and another thirty-two cases in which electronic "bugging" devices were installed by CIA agents.

In its report, the Rockefeller commission made thirty recommendations intended to prevent future abuses by the CIA. It is suggested, for example, that the two houses of Congress appoint a joint committee to oversee CIA operations in place of four subcommittees that were accused of inadequate supervision in the past. It also recommended that Congress consider making public the CIA's long-secret budget in the future in order to eliminate "one of the underlying causes of the problems confronting the CIA." In addition, the commission suggested a number of changes that would tighten internal controls over CIA employees.

Meanwhile, committees of the House and Senate have launched their own investigations of the CIA. It is likely that these investigations will uncover still further abuses and witch-hunting activities.

Aside from carrying out programs that ultimately led to investigations of alleged governmental misconduct, the Nixon administration employed other means to try to suppress political dissent. One such means was the criminal prosecution of members of left-wing groups on conspiracy charges. In several trials, the evidence showed that major roles in the alleged conspiracies had actually been played by paid informers for the government.

A typical case involved a group called the "Camden Twenty-eight"—composed of antiwar activists, including Catholic priests and laymen, in Camden, New Jersey. The twenty-eight members of the group, who opposed the military draft, were arrested in 1971 on charges of conspiracy, of breaking into a draft board office, and of destroying draft records. Testimony at their 1973 trial disclosed that the prime mover in the plan to raid the draft board office had been a paid FBI informer, Robert W. Hardy, who testified: "This raid on the draft board would not have happened without me and the FBI."

Much of Hardy's testimony was confirmed by FBI agents. The agent in charge of the case, Joseph Ziel, testified it was standard procedure for the FBI to permit an informer "to be active within the group that he is working with"—even to the point of providing expertise and supplies.

Defense attorneys argued that Hardy had been not merely an informer, but an agent provocateur—that is, someone hired to incite an illegal act. The jurors apparently agreed. They found the defendants not guilty.

A second case involved another antiwar group known as the "Gainesville Eight"—composed of seven members of an organization called Vietnam Veterans Against the War and one of their supporters. They were tried in 1973 in Gainesville, Florida, on charges of conspiring to disrupt the 1972 Republican National Convention in Miami Beach. The government charged that members of the organization had planned to shoot high-powered slingshots at policemen guarding the Republican convention site. They hoped, the prosecution claimed, that such attacks would provoke the police into assaulting other, peaceful demonstrators who would be present. The veterans then planned to fire automatic weapons at police stations, stores, and power lines in Miami in attempts to lure the police away from the convention site so that the men with the slingshots could escape, the government said.

The defendants were arrested before the convention began, and no such attacks were ever made. The chief government witnesses were five paid FBI informers who had infiltrated Vietnam Veterans Against the War—several of whom admitted proposing that the group engage in violent protests.

Defense lawyers argued that the government had manufactured the charges against the "Gainesville Eight" in an attempt to discredit the antiwar movement. The jurors found all the defendants not guilty.

Similar trials—involving groups that came to be known by such names as the "Evanston Four," the "Seattle Seven," and the "Kansas City Four"—also ended with verdicts of not guilty. But the Nixon administration continued its efforts to harass left-wing groups.

Army intelligence agents maintained the policy begun during the Johnson administration of investigating civilians they suspected of subversive activities. Senator Ervin introduced a bill in 1974 to prohibit military authorities from conducting such surveillances. The bill provided that any military man found guilty of such spying could be sent to prison for up to two years and fined up to $10,000. The Nixon administration opposed the Ervin measure. Although Ervin retired from the Senate in 1975, his bill is still under consideration at this writing.

The Nixon administration tried to push through Congress legislation of its own aimed at further restricting the rights of Americans. One such measure was intended to limit citizens' rights to travel to foreign countries. It was apparently inspired by embarrassment caused the Nixon government when some of its critics, such as antiwar activist and actress Jane Fonda, visited North Vietnam and other foreign countries and made statements assailing administration policies. The bill would make it a crime, punishable by up to five years in prison, for an American to defy an order by the secretary of state to refrain from visiting a foreign nation "to which travel would impair United States foreign policy." The measure would also provide criminal penalties for visiting a forbidden nation that was at war, experiencing insurrection or armed hostilities, or "engaged in armed conflict with the United States." All the government would have to do to restrict travel to such a country would be to designate it in writing as a forbidden visitation area.

Another means used by the Nixon administration to curb dissent was the withholding of federal scholarship funds from college students arrested during protest demonstrations.

Students have been the targets of other recent government actions tending to inhibit dissent. For example, in 1970 a nineteen-year-old girl, Debra Sweet of Madison, Wisconsin, was one of a group of students presented National Young Americans medals for achievement by President Nixon at a White House ceremony. Miss Sweet used the occasion to tell the president that she doubted his sincerity "until you get us out of Vietnam." As a result of the embarrassment caused Nixon, the FBI began conducting background investigations on all students nominated for such awards, as well as those who helped select the nominees.

In 1971, the Senate Internal Security Subcommittee became embroiled in controversy when it accepted for its official files a collection of reports on 125,000 supposedly subversive persons and groups that had been put together by a private vigilante organization. The reports had been gathered by a group headed by retired U.S. Army Major General Ralph Van Denman of San Diego, California. Between his retirement in 1929 and his death in 1952, he had devoted most of his time to collecting dossiers on individuals and organizations he considered subversive. He had an extensive network of informants throughout the country—private citizens who fed him vast amounts of raw, unverified data, some of which was as much as forty years old.

Critics of the Internal Security Subcommittee charged that the acceptance of the files was irresponsible, but the subcommittee defended its acceptance of the files: "They were examined and found pertinent and germane to the subcommittee's purposes."

The House Un-American Activities Committee also remained controversial. It changed its name in 1969 to the House Internal Security Committee, but its tactics did not vary from those of the past.

In October 1970, the House committee stirred a furor by releasing a list of what it described as sixty-five "radical" campus speakers. The committee first sent out a questionnaire to 179 colleges and universities across the country, asking them to report all speakers who had appeared on their campuses during the previous two years. Ninety-five of the schools complied with the request, listing not only the speakers but the fees they had been paid for their talks. Precisely what qualified a person to be ranked as a "radical" was not explained, but the committee also released a list of organizations with which it said the "radical" speakers were affiliated. Among the speakers were John Ciardi, poetry editor of the *Saturday Review* magazine; the Reverend John C. Bennett, former president of Union Theological Seminary in New York; Dr. Benjamin Spock, the pediatrician; and the Reverend Wyatt T. Walker, a former aide to the late Dr. Martin Luther King, Jr.

The American Civil Liberties Union filed a lawsuit seeking to prohibit the House committee from publishing its list of supposed "radicals," arguing that such publication would violate the right of free speech and harass the persons listed. As a result, Judge Gerhard A. Gesell of the U.S. District Court in Washington issued an injunction barring publication of the list.

Gesell ruled that the list and an accompanying committee report had no "proper legislative purpose and infringes on the rights of the individuals named therein." He said that it would be "illegal" to publish the report at public expense, and that the report intended "to inhibit further speech on college campuses by those listed individuals and others whose political persuasion is not in accord with that of members of the committee."

To get around Judge Gesell's order, the House committee prepared a slightly revised version of its original report. Congressman Richard Ichord, who had become chairman of the committee, then asked the full House to pass a resolution prohibiting judges or anyone else from obstructing the printing and public distribution of the revised report. The resolution was approved. Since Gesell's injunction applied only to the original committee report, it could not be used to block publication of the revised report. As no effort was made to obtain a similar injunction against the revised report, it was printed and distributed at government expense.

During the late 1960s and early 1970s, two members of Congress who opposed the tactics used by the House Internal Security Committee obtained membership on the committee. Democratic Congressman Louis Stokes of Ohio served on the committee in 1969 and 1970. He was replaced as a member in 1971 by Democratic Congressman Robert F. Drinan of Massachusetts, a Catholic priest who had been elected to the House the previous year. Although their efforts to curb the witch-hunting activities were initially unsuccessful, they did at least provide criticism of the committee's actions from the inside. However, Drinan's 1971 proposal that the committee be abolished was voted down; and his 1974 fight to cripple the committee by cutting off its funds was defeated.

In November 1974, however, many conservative congressmen who had long supported the Internal Security Committee lost their seats in the elections to more liberal candidates. When the new Congress convened in January 1975, Drinan led another effort to abolish the committee. This time, the campaign was successful. The Internal Security Committee files and some of its staff members were shifted to the Judiciary Committee.

Although the Judiciary Committee has had a generally responsible reputation over the years, there is no guarantee that it will refrain from conducting future witch hunts of the kind for which the Internal Security Committee and its predecessor, HUAC, became notorious. In the other house of Congress, the Senate Internal Security Subcommittee—which has its own long record of witch-hunt activities—remains in existence and continues to function in much the same manner as in past years.

Members of the executive and legislative branches of the federal government have not been alone in taking part in recent witch-hunt activities. Officials of local school districts, colleges, and universities, for instance, have been involved in a number of purges of teachers with controversial backgrounds. Ira Glasser, executive director of the New York chapter of the ACLU, said his organization recently has experienced a "resurgence" of complaints about political reprisals against teachers. There is "a growing trend of political purges of teachers," he said. Glasser noted that his office was receiving formal complaints at the rate of about a half dozen a week—"more than at any time since the McCarthy era"—from teachers who charged that their academic freedom has been threatened because of their political beliefs.

Ironically, after speaking out publicly on the problem, Glasser himself became a victim of the trend. In addition to carrying out his ACLU duties, he held a part-time teaching position at New York University. In April 1974, he was fired from the teaching job because he refused to sign an oath swearing that he would uphold the New York State and U.S. Constitutions. Glasser said he objected to the oath because "it's exacting a gesture of obeisance to the state as a requirement of teaching." The course Glasser had been teaching before his dismissal was "The Repressive Society."

Another area of recent witch-hunting activities involved secret investigations and collection of extensive dossiers by local and state law-enforcement agencies on persons with unpopular political beliefs. In Oklahoma, for example, it was disclosed that a little-known state agency had secretly collected files on 6,000 persons considered potential "troublemakers."

Stephen Jones, an attorney for the Oklahoma Civil Liberties Union, said the blacklist had been used to prevent numerous black and white persons who had taken part in peace rallies and civil-rights demonstrations from obtaining jobs, and it had also been used to bar activist students from enrollment in a state university. A lawsuit seeking destruction of the files has not yet come to trial.

A similar suit filed by sixteen political activists in New York, which is also pending, resulted in the disclosure that the New York City Police Department maintained political-intelligence files on 1,220,000 persons and 125,000 organizations. After the suit was filed, the department announced that it was destroying the out-of-date dossiers on 980,000 of the individuals and 100,000 of the organizations. Attorneys for the sixteen activists criticized the fact that the department was still maintaining files on 240,000 persons and 25,000 organizations. "To purge the files of people and organizations that have long since died or disappeared is of no use to citizens whose privacy is under attack today," the lawyers said in a prepared statement.

Such files also were gathered by other law-enforcement agencies across the country. Since the units collecting the information usually operated with utmost secrecy, persons under investigation often had no idea that dossiers were being compiled about them.

These circumstances point up the problems of coping

[270]

with the witch-hunt philosophy. Innocent persons not only can be victimized by unseen forces, but can be victimized without even knowing the forces exist.

SOURCES AND SUPPLEMENTARY READING

Background information on Richard Nixon's political career before his election to the presidency can be found in *Richard Nixon: A Political and Personal Portrait* by Earl Mazo (Harper and Brothers, 1959) and *The Strange Case of Richard Milhous Nixon* by Jerry Voorhis (Popular Library, 1973).

Much information about witch-hunting activities carried out by the federal government during Nixon's White House years was uncovered by the Senate Select Committee on Presidential Campaign Activities. The voluminous transcripts and reports of the committee were extremely valuable in my research, as were interviews with committee members and staff personnel. The House Judiciary Committee, which conducted its own investigation of witch-hunt activities in considering Nixon's impeachment, also issued useful transcripts and reports.

The reports of the House Internal Security Committee, especially the 1971 annual report containing the "supplemental view" of Congressman Robert F. Drinan, were valuable in outlining the differing political philosophies within the committee and the efforts made to curb its witch-hunt activities. The committee's report on supposed "radical campus speakers" was supplemented by news accounts of the controversy surrounding its release.

SUMMING UP

"If there is any fixed star in our constitutional constellation, it is that no official, high or petty, can prescribe what shall be orthodox in politics, nationalism, religion or other matters of opinion, or force citizens to confess by word or act their faith therein." Those words were contained in a 1943 United States Supreme Court decision written by Justice Robert H. Jackson. They summarize succinctly and well the American tradition that is violated by the witch hunt mania.

Witch hunts are designed to expose and punish those whose ideas stray from the orthodox. They play on the fears of the populace—most notably the fear that opinions differing from those of the nation's majority are potentially dangerous. They claim to be protecting "Americanism." But true Americanism recognizes the need to respect the widest possible range of ideas and to defend even the most unpopular of opinions. Our government was not founded by men who held or permitted only one view; it

[272]

was founded by men with diverse backgrounds and philosophies who wrote into the Constitution provisions guaranteeing broad freedom of thought and expression.

The necessity for preserving that freedom was emphasized in the fall of 1953, at the height of the McCarthy era, in a speech by former President Harry S Truman. Addressing a dinner of the Four Freedoms Foundation, Truman said:

> The good life is not possible without freedom. But only the people, by their will and by their dedication to freedom, can make the good life come to pass. We cannot leave it to the courts alone, because many of the invasions of these freedoms are so devious and so subtle that they cannot be brought before the courts.
>
> The responsibility for these freedoms falls on free men. And free men can preserve them only if they are militant about freedom. We ought to get angry when these rights are violated, and make ourselves heard until the wrong is righted. . . . There are times when the defense of freedom calls for vigorous action. This action may lead to trouble, and frequently does. Effective effort to preserve freedom may involve discomfort and risk. It takes faith, unselfishness and courage to stand up to a bully; or to stand up for a whole community when it has been frightened into subjection. But it has to be done if we are to remain free.
>
> We have to start wherever we can—in the family, the lodge, the business community, the union, our local government, party, church—and work outward; asserting, demanding, insisting that the most

[273]

unpopular persons are entitled to all the freedoms, to fundamental fairness. Almost always, the issues are raised over unpopular people or unpopular causes. In the cause of freedom, we have to battle for the rights of people with whom we do not agree and whom, in many cases, we may not like. These people test the strength of the freedoms which protect all of us. If we do not defend their rights, we endanger our own.

Those rights remain endangered today, for despite warnings such as those issued by Truman and others who have followed him, the witch-hunt philosophy persists. One of the peculiar aspects of this philosophy is that it seems to assume the United States is so insecure it cannot stand up to the test of being challenged by controversial doctrines.

Another disturbing characteristic of the witch-hunt movement is its emphasis on viewing matters of loyalty from the negative, rather than positive, perspective. This factor was effectively described by author Alan Barth in *The Loyalty of Free Men.*

"Loyalty" has become a cult, an obsession, in the United States. . . . It is thought of not so much in terms of an affirmative faith in the great purposes for which the American nation was created as in terms of stereotypes, the mere questioning of which is deemed "disloyal." The whole . . . accent is on something called "un-Americanism"—a hyphenated synonym for unorthodoxy. . . . "Loyalty" consists today in not being un-American, which is to say in not being different or individualistic. The very diversity which was the wellspring of loyalty in the past is now distrusted.

Throughout this book, we have seen how individual targets of witch hunts have been victimized. The long list of ruined reputations, wrecked careers, broken lives—even suicides—speaks eloquently about the evils of the witch-hunt philosophy. But the broader factor of the effect on the public at large must also be considered. When Americans are afraid to speak their minds, when they look with unwarranted suspicion at their neighbors, when they fear to give fair consideration to unpopular ideas, the national spirit suffers incalculable damage.

As the late radio news analyst Elmer Davis wrote in *But We Were Born Free:* "This republic was not established by cowards; and cowards will not preserve it."

ACKNOWLEDGMENTS

I deeply appreciate the cooperation given me by officials of the U.S. House Internal Security Committee, the Senate Internal Security Subcommittee, the Senate Government Operations Committee, the White House, the Justice Department, the FBI, the Subversive Activities Control Board, and the American Civil Liberties Union. Although some of these officials were aware that my book was bound to be critical of their organizations, they nonetheless helped smooth the path of my research.

To Ron Buehl, Cary Ryan, and Dorothy Markinko, my gratitude for counsel and patience. And to Marilynn Meeker, my thanks for painstaking, faithful editing of the book.

To my wife, Jeanne, and daughters, Pamela and Patricia, my thanks once again for enduring the deprivations of life with a writer.

Numerous books provided valuable information. Among the most helpful were:

Andrews, Bert and Peter, *A Tragedy of History*. Washington, D.C.: Robert B. Luce, Inc., 1962.

Barth, Alan, *The Loyalty of Free Men.* New York: Viking Press, 1951.

Bentley Eric, editor, *Thirty Years of Treason.* New York: Viking Press, 1971.

Buckley, William F., Jr., *The Committee and Its Critics.* New York: G. P. Putnam's Sons, 1962.

Cook, Fred J., *The Nightmare Decade.* New York: Random House, 1971.

Davis, Elmer, *But We Were Born Free.* Indianapolis: Bobbs-Merrill, 1954.

Donner, Frank J., *The Un-Americans.* New York: Ballantine, 1961.

Faulk, John Henry, *Fear on Trial.* New York: Simon and Schuster, 1964.

Goodman, Walter, *The Committee.* New York: Farrar, Straus and Giroux, 1968.

Kanfer, Stefan, *A Journal of the Plague Years.* New York: Atheneum, 1973.

Kempton, Murray, *Part of Our Time.* New York: Simon and Schuster, 1955.

Nixon, Richard M., *Six Crises.* Garden City, N.Y.: Doubleday, 1962.

Potter, Charles E., *Days of Shame.* New York: Coward, McCann and Geoghegan, 1965.

Rovere, Richard H., *Senator Joe McCarthy.* New York: Harcourt, Brace, 1959.

Taylor, Telford, *Grand Inquest.* New York: Simon and Schuster, 1955.

Thomas, Lately, *When Even Angels Wept.* New York: William Morrow, 1973.

Wechsler, James, *The Age of Suspicion.* New York: Random House, 1953.

[277]

INDEX

Johnson, Lyndon B. (cont'd.)
  Pentagon demonstration
    (1967) and, 240–241
Johnson, Dr. Robert L., 187, 196
Joint Anti-Fascist Refugee Committee, 55–56
Jolson Story, The, (motion picture), 82
Jones, Stephen, 270
Jonkel, Jon M., 170
Journal of the American Bar Association, 178
Justice Department Internal Security Division, 252–253
Justice Department scandals, 14

"Kansas City Four," 264
Kaplan, Raymond, 185
Kazan, Elia, 86–87
Kefauver, Estes, 14
Kennedy, Edward M., 256
Kennedy, John F., 15, 184, 231–236, 252
Kennedy, Robert F., 232
Kenny, Robert, 68
Kenyon, Dorothy, 153–154
Kerr, Jean, 171
Kerr, John, 42, 43
Kerr committee, 42–44
King, Dr. Martin Luther, Jr., 242, 244, 267
Kinoy, Arthur, 237, 238
Knowles, Mary, 221
Knox, Henry, 11–12
Kohler, Walter, 181
Korean War, 207
Kramer, Charles, 105, 108
Kraus, Charles A., 143, 144

Lackland Air Force Base, 225
LaFollette, Philip, 140
LaFollette, Robert M., 140
LaFollette, Robert M., Jr., 140–141
Lardner, Ring, Jr., 68, 75–77, 82

Lattimore, Owen, 157–162, 181
  "McCarthyism" and, 160
Lawson, John Howard, 68–73, 75, 77
Lewisburg Federal Prison, 130
Liberation, 245
Lindsay, John V., 256
Lodge, Henry Cabot, Jr., 152, 161, 164, 165
Loeb, Philip, 81
Lovett, Robert M., 42–45
Lowell, Robert, 240
Loyalty of Free Men, The (Barth), 274–275
Loyalty investigations, 224–225
Loyalty Review Board, 61
Lucas, Scott, 148, 149, 151, 152, 173

MacArthur, General Douglas, 162
McCarthy, Joseph R., 1–4, 133–217, 219, 273
  anticommunism as major re-election issue, 143–144
  appears before Senate to answer charges, 148–151
  background of, 134–136
  Benton and, 176–182
  Budenz and, 161, 162
  Butler and, 170–174
  calls for Senate investigation, 151–152
  campaigns for U.S. Senate, 139–142
  censured by Senate, 216
  CIA and, 201–202
  Cohn and, 182–188, 202–215
  controversy over his first Senate election, 141–142
  death of, 217
  "Declaration of Conscience" against, 162–164, 178
  early Senate record, 142–143
  education of, 134

U.S. State Department, McCarthy and, 133–196
U.S. Supreme Court, 44–45
U.S. Treasury Department (1800 and 1824), 13–14
Universal Pictures, 91

Vail, Richard, 57
Van Denman, Major General Ralph, 266
Vassar College, 23, 99–100
Vaughn, David B., 38–39
Velde, Harold H., 84
Veterans Affairs Committee, 51, 52
Vietnam Veterans Against the War, 263, 264
"Voice of America" (radio program), 183–186
Voorhis, Jerry, 251–252

Walker, Reverend Wyatt T., 267
Wallace, Henry A., 37–38
Walsh, Reverend Edmund, 143, 144
Walter, Francis E., 219–232, 235
Walter-McCarran Act (1952), 219
Walters, Basil, 193
Wanderer (Hayden), 86
Ware, Harold, 102–103
Washington, George, 8–12
Washington Post, 121
Washington Times-Herald, 170, 171
Watergate scandal, ix–xi, 15, 257–271
Watkins, Arthur, 215

Watkins committee, McCarthy and, 215–216
Watson, Goodwin, 36, 42–45
Watson, Thomas J., Jr., 257
WCBS radio, 90
Wechsler, James, 188–194
Welsh, George, 32
Wheeler, William, 125, 126, 227
Wheeling Intelligencer, 144–145
Wherry, Kenneth, 150–151
Wiesner, Dr. Jerome B., 184
Wiley, Alexander, 139
Wilkins, Roy, 222
Willis, Edwin, 235–236, 240
Wilson, Dagmar, 233, 235
Wilson, Edmund, 194
Witch hunt, definition of, ix
Witt, Nathan, 105, 108
Women Strike for Peace, 233–235, 261
Wood, John, 53–55, 57, 82, 89
Woodcock, Leonard, 257
Works Progress Administration (WPA), 22, 24
World War II, 14, 34–35, 37, 52, 54, 85, 100, 146, 158, 175
  McCarthy and, 136–139
Wulf, Melvin, 254
Wurf, Jerry, 257

Young Communist League (YCL), 188, 190, 192, 193
Youth International Party (Yippies), 245

Zeidler, Carl, 136–137, 139
Ziel, Joseph, 263
Zwicker, Brigadier General Ralph, 208–216